The Here Guide to

Management

M000048052

The Heretic's Guide to Management

The Art of Harnessing Ambiguity

PAUL CULMSEE

AND

KAILASH AWATI

The Heretic's Guide to Management
The Art of Harnessing Ambiguity

Copyright © 2016 by Paul Culmsee and Kailash Awati

All rights reserved. No part of this book may be used or reproduced by any means, graphic, electronic, or mechanical, including photocopying, recording, taping or by any information storage retrieval system without the express written permission of the publisher except for the use of brief quotations in a book review or scholarly journal.

While the publisher and the authors have used good faith efforts to ensure that the information contained in this work is accurate, the publisher and authors disclaim all responsibility for error or omissions, including without limitation, responsibility for damages resulting from the use of or reliance on this work. Use of the information contained in this work is at your own risk.

Because of the dynamic nature of the Internet, any web addresses or links contained in this book may have changed since publication and may no longer be valid.

ISBN: 978-0-9946314-0-4 (e-book)
ISBN: 978-0-9946314-1-1 (paperback)
ISBN: 978-0-9946314-2-8 (hardcover)

Heretics Guide Press
PO Box 3816
Marsfield NSW 2122
Australia
www.hereticsguidebooks.com
First Printing: 2016

Contents

Acknowledgements

Paul:

To my colleagues/friends/collaborators who either influenced or helped shape this book. In no particular order, John Robertson, Mike Kapitola, Neil Preston, Andrew Jolly, Chris Tomich, Peter Chow, Du Le, Bill Cullen, Paul Taplin, Robert Bogue, Lou Zulli, Simon Buckingham-Shum, Lee Horn, Ryan Scott, Arthur Shelley, Vanessa Oats, Margot Wood, William Wardlaw Rogers, Jeff Conklin, KC. Burgess Yakemovic, and Jess Steele.

To my father, Mike Culmsee, who once again reviewed the manuscript and made us take out our excessive use of parentheses.

Especially to my wife Terrie and my wonderful kids, Ashlee and Liam. For their support, feedback and patience.

Kailash:

Management books tend to draw heavily on the experiences of their authors. This book is no exception. To this end, I've been fortunate to interact with a large number of individuals who drew my attention to some of the paradoxes and subtleties of managing ambiguity. They are too numerous to mention by name so I'd like to take this opportunity to thank them collectively.

A big thank you to Sashi Gundlapalli, Ravin Kurian, Anh Vu, Yasuhiro Nishimi, Deon Pieterse, En-Hao Chua, Gerhard Kraus, Marcelo Grasso, Sean Heffernan, Vlado Bokan, Shang-Lin Koh, Anusha, Alexis-Ann Dizon and Joe Helo for their help and support over the last few years.

It is my pleasure to acknowledge interesting conversations on ambiguity and other matters with Chris Tomich, Simon Buckingham-Shum and Karuna Ramanathan.

I've benefited from the ongoing support of numerous friends from the BITS Pilani alumni community. Thanks guys ... and I know you'll all forgive me for not calling you out by name.

Finally, and most crucially, my deepest appreciation to Arati, Rohan and Vikram who, quite unambiguously, make it all worthwhile.

Paul and Kailash:

We have to call out one person in particular. Ashlee Culmsee, a very skilled and talented artist whose wonderful work graces not only the cover of this book, but all of the diagrams throughout. In between study for final year exams, she still managed to not only bring our ideas to life, but give them a character all their own. Thank you so much, Ashlee. You did an outstanding job!

Preface

The first thing that will strike anyone who has read (or even just browsed) our previous book is this one is considerably shorter. This is deliberate: after churning out a book that ended up being 411 pages, this time around we wanted to create something a little less like a double quarter-pounder with extra cheese. In keeping with that, we will be equally brief with this preface.

Our first book, *The Heretics Guide to Best Practices*, was written five years ago (three years ago if you count the reprint). In between, a lot changed for us professionally: Kailash moved to Singapore to set up an IT Service Centre and Paul had a go at the world of start-up companies. In that time, we spoke to each other regularly, and one of the topics that kept coming up in our conversations was that we should do another book. The basic theme presented itself gradually through our almost daily experiences in dealing with *ambiguity*.

Most management techniques aim to reduce or eliminate ambiguity. Unfortunately, they usually suck at it and somewhat ironically, often increase it. This is reflected in a tragedy that plays out over and over again: a new technique or approach promises plenty, but when applied, delivers much less and ends up being labelled a fad.

Although most fads start out as legitimate efforts to *finally* get things organised, they all seem to come undone because of inherent contradictions that become apparent only after they've been around for a while. There is good reason for this: management techniques deal with what can be seen—the external manifestations of thoughts, actions and events. By and large, they do not address the effect that ambiguity has on people's thoughts, intentions and behaviours.

But this is precisely where the problem is. Unless one understands ambiguity and its effects on individuals, it is highly unlikely that *any* management method will get anywhere at all.

In this book, we place *ambiguity* centre stage, and do so in a way that we hope you will find both informative and entertaining. Like our previous book, there is irreverence and humour, but be warned that you may have your cherished beliefs tested. Ah, and as the cover suggests, you'll likely meet a few teddy bears along the way, teddies you will probably recognise as being tightly held by your colleagues and friends.

Enough said! We hope you're intrigued enough to read on.

Paul and Kailash (Perth/Sydney, June 2016)

The Heretics Guide to

Management

1

Six Easy Steps...

Guru: Hey! Who wants to get rich today?
Homer Simpson: (among a chorus of voices): Me! Me! - Me! Me! Me!
Me! I said it first.
Guru projects a picture of a pyramid on a flipchart marked with a red cross
Guru: "Let me assure you that this is not one of those "shady" pyramid
schemes you've been hearing about..."
Guru replaces pyramid picture with projects a modified one with a flattened top
Guru: Our model is the trapezoid that guarantees each investor an 800%
return within hours of your initial...
Sirens blare in the distance...
Guru: Uh-oh! The cops!
Guru jumps out of the window...

Introduction

We are going to start this book with an "ice-breaker" activity—the kind that facilitators do when starting a workshop, to get people in the right frame of mind for the work ahead. Of course, we realise this doesn't quite translate to the solitary task of book reading, but we request you go with it anyway ... we will be asking you to "go with it" a few more times in this book so this is a good opportunity to get used to it.

Let's determine what your supermodel *catwalk name* is. The process is simple: take the name of your first ever pet, append to it the name of the street you first lived on, and there you have it ... your model name. For the record, Paul's is "Teo Kingsfold" and Kailash's "Goldie Minns".

Now you might well be wondering about the point of that exercise. It is that we want to let you in on the best kept secret about how to "make it" in the competitive world of management consulting (or selling pyramid marketing schemes for that matter). If you really want to hit the big time, you need to *create a management model, market it well and hope like hell that it catches on.* If it does, then you go from a small-time model pusher to a big-time guru, because you would have succeeded in creating a "supermodel" and be well on your way to creating a new *management fashion.* For smart consultants, this is brilliant because it comes with all the trappings of thought leadership fame, including a LinkedIn group dedicated to your model, guaranteed keynote slots at conferences, trademarked training and glossy certifications at thousands of dollars a pop—all to sustain an ever burgeoning community of fans.

For the average corporate minion trying to navigate the sometimes complex maze of work (which includes all you managers out there), management models are hugely helpful because they offer a means to make sense of an organisational reality that can otherwise feel overwhelming. Such conceptual or logical models are at the very foundation of how we humans understand and solve problems. They help us interpret and understand what we are experiencing and equally important, enable us to convey that understanding to others. Indeed, most of our beliefs about what is right, and our consequent actions, are based on models that we have learnt in the course of our lives. In particular, managers' beliefs about how their professional world works and how they should respond to it are influenced by models that they learn on the job, in business schools, through industry certifications or in books written by management gurus whose models have caught on.

From the purely commercial perspective of an aspiring thought leader, models also play a critical role: getting people to part with their cash...

Six easy steps...

The trick to marketing a good management formula or recipe has a lot in common with marketing in the cosmetics industry. For example: just about all skin care products have an attention-grabbing name and a unique "secret" formula or ingredient that is guaranteed to make wrinkles disappear in a few short applications. Similarly, the glossy brochures and webinars of consultancies seek to persuade you that *their* model is far superior to the lame one promoted by their competitors down the road. As a bonus, they claim that it offers a sure-fire formula for making organisational wrinkles disappear.

So if you accept that you need a model with a catchy name to make it in the big bad world of corporate consulting, we can demonstrate the value of this book in just a few paragraphs.

How? Well, hold on to your hat: we are about to demonstrate—in six easy steps[1]—just how easy it is to come up with your own consulting model.

1. Determine your model name (you have already done that!)
2. Pick a number between 3 and 5
3. Pick a noun like: steps, pillars, forces, elements, processes, waves, boxes or hats
4. Pick an adjective like: outstanding, breakthrough, innovative, unleashing, releasing
5. Pick a noun from: team, organisation or community

---

[1] Yes, we realise we are peddling a model to make fun of other models. Rest assured this is quite deliberate (and will occur regularly throughout this book)

6. Pick a noun like: excellence, energy, performance, strategy, change, efficiency, collaboration, dynamics

Now put the words together using the template below:

"The [1] [2] [3] model for [4] [5] [6]"

Armed with these steps, we hereby present...

"The Goldie Minns 4 forces model for breakthrough team energy" (Kailash)
"The Teo Kingsfold 3 pillars model for outstanding organisation strategy" (Paul)

Now you have your very own consulting model, but you are only halfway there. The next step is getting the right "look" by drawing an appropriate diagram to capture your wisdom in a catchy visual form. Remember that legions of potential followers will be drawing this diagram for others, so it's important not to overdo the make-up. It has to be simple, memorable and easy to draw on a whiteboard or PowerPoint presentation. Thus we strongly recommend going with a "natural look" by using a common shape like a pyramid, 2*2 matrix or a Venn diagram. Complex shapes like dodecahedrons are to be avoided at all costs.

To guide you on the creation of your model, in Figure 1.1 we have provided a convenient table of fashionable shapes to work with. Ultimately, the look you go for depends on what random number and noun you picked in Steps 2 and 3. For example, a 2*2 matrix is only good if you chose 4, so if you really like the "Midnight SWOT" look but only have 3 forces, throw in another factor to your model. If you chose "pillars" in Step 3, you could go with the "Pyramid Noir" or "Pillar Chic" look, depending on whether your model is hierarchical or not.

Also, be sure to add some arrows here and there if you can ... people like arrows.

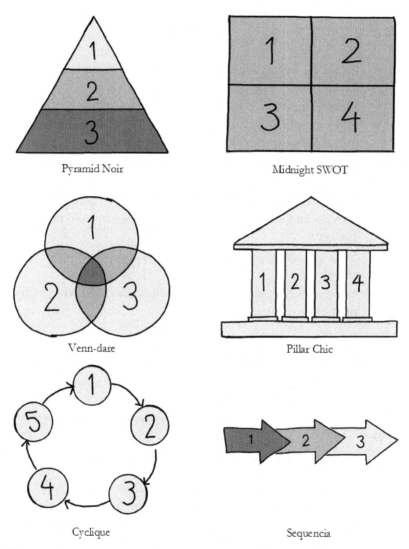

Pyramid Noir

Midnight SWOT

Venn-dare

Pillar Chic

Cyclique

Sequencia

Figure 1.1: Recommended supermodel archetypes

The penultimate step is to write a whitepaper or better, a small book, that expands on the model. The key to writing such a book is you need to follow the management fashion checklist. Borrowing from Matthews

(2015), you need to ensure your book meets some or all of the following criteria:

- Create the perception that your remedies are simple and easy to implement.
- Provide prescriptive answers to complex issues and problems.
- Offer the promise of quick wins followed by bigger benefits in the longer term.
- Claim universality—that your model applies to all organisations at all times.
- Target specific contemporary issues (at the time of writing, mergers and acquisitions, big data analytics and the internet of things).
- Make it seemingly novel, but don't provide overly radical answers.
- Garner the support of recognised individuals who actively promote your ideas.

The final, most important step of model making is to have a good backstory as to what inspired the model in the first place. This is critical because if your model is to succeed in the long run, it needs a memorable story or anecdote to guarantee it a place in management folklore. After all, just look at what a falling apple did for Sir Isaac Newton!

If you do not have a compelling backstory yet, we advise you stick to one of the following tried and tested winners:

- "I had a Eureka moment and I now have these profound insights…"
- "I have uniquely worked closely with the leaders of thousands of successful companies and had these profound insights…"
- "This company has outperformed everyone—and I have worked out their secret…"

One last tip: don't be afraid to add in some personal embarrassment to a good "profound insight" story either. Archimedes pioneered that one over three thousand years ago when he allegedly ran naked through the streets shouting "Eureka!" Thus "I stubbed my toe on the doorstep and had a profound realisation…" is absolutely legit.

And there you have it. Armed with our framework, you can now come up with a model of your very own, add it to the existing management model zoo and travel the international guru speaker circuit, telling the story of how it came about. With a bit of luck, you will soon be well on your way to management gurudom.

Mine is more right than yours…

Okay, so we are exaggerating just a teensy bit, but in all seriousness, many disciplines are drowning in various models making their claims to rightness. Management in particular has hundreds, if not thousands, to choose from and we have listed but a sub-microscopic subset below. While their titles are not quite as extravagant as our formula-generated ones (and neither are we suggesting that they are in any way as flippant) the list nevertheless tells an interesting story:

- Hannan and Freeman "Structural Inertia Model" for Organisational Change
- Kurt Lewin's "unfreezing-change-refreeze" Change Model
- Bruch and Ghoshal's model for Unleashing Organisational Energy
- Browns Collective Social Learning Spiral
- Prosci ADKAR model for Change Management
- Nadler and Tushman's Congruence Model for Organization Analysis
- Falletta's Organizational Intelligence Model
- McKinsey 7S Framework
- Weisbord's Six-Box Model
- Kotter's 8-Step Change Model

The aforementioned list focuses just on models in the area of organisational change and its close cousin, organisational development. The question that comes to mind when one sees this list of organisational change models is: *why are there so many?* Surely, if there is one right or best way to do it, as consultancies and gurus often claim, then as time goes on, we ought to converge to a small set of variables (and models) that result in a consistent pattern of reduced "organisational wrinkles". This would enable us to work towards that ideal single model or fundamental management law to rule them all.

However, to this day, theories and models of change keep popping up with frightening frequency in respected journals like *The Journal of Organizational Change Management* and *Harvard Business Review* (not to mention the overcrowded business section shelf of your local bookstore where we hope you found this book!) Furthermore, many consultancies, taking a cue from academics, offer their own trademarked change models which they claim are proven by practice. Irrespective of the source, all of them have reassuring names that offer you four steps, five pillars or six forces to enable organisational or change enlightenment.

The fact that there are so many models of change seems to suggest that a model (like talk!) is cheap. Armed with a whiteboard and sufficient time, it is easy enough to build one. It is also fun given that you get to sit around a whiteboard all day and feel like you have done something productive, despite having solved no real-life problems at all. Academics and their students who spend years developing models would take issue with this statement and rightfully argue that it is not quite that simple: considerable brain power, experimentation, data gathering, testing and reflection goes into developing theories and models. Even so, one can't help but wonder why, despite all the collective wisdom and experience of countless distinguished academics and practitioners, we are no closer to finding that one best practice or management model to rule them all.

The most famous model ever

One could make a case that one of the first human supermodels was Lisa del Giocondo, better known as the lady in the Mona Lisa painting by Leonardo da Vinci. Hers is, after all, one of the most recognisable faces in the world. Each year, more than 6 million people visit the Louvre in France to see her. Here is a picture of the Mona Lisa for you to enjoy...

Figure 1.2: A model of the Mona Lisa

Looking at the picture in Figure 1.2, we clearly see this is not the original but a paint-by-numbers model of the Mona Lisa—a *representation* of the original. The implicit claim made with a model like this is that by filling in the numbered areas with the right colours, you too could have your very own Mona Lisa.

What do you think? If we painted this model, would it look like the real Mona Lisa?

Unlikely! As everyone instinctively realises, it would probably look as amateurish as a finger painting. Yet, in many ways, this is precisely what all models seek to do. Like our Mona Lisa example, the (oft unstated) implication of any model is if you follow all the instructions listed, success will be assured. However, unlike the Mona Lisa example, many people are blind to the fact that "painting by numbers" on management models will also result in substandard, and in many cases, even undesirable outcomes.

There are a couple of issues afflicting both the Mona Lisa and management paint-by-numbers models. We need to recognise that models are simplifications of reality. Model-makers look at the real "thing" being modelled and attempt to analyse it by breaking it up into what they think are its constituent components. In the Mona Lisa example, someone has looked at the colours and shapes of the original and used that as a basis to create a model of it. In the case of management, academics and consultants attempt to capture the essence of real-world organisations by extracting and representing the key features that they believe are important.

But here's the thing ... it would have taken Leonardo da Vinci *years* to master the *craft* of painting and along that journey there would have been many missteps and refinements to his technique. So there is much more to the Mona Lisa than the painting alone. It represents Da Vinci's *journey of learning*. Such a journey cannot be represented by anything other than the original and even that won't tell you why Da Vinci chose a certain colour or brush stroke. Nor will it show you all of the false starts, missteps and crappy paintings that came before and ultimately *enabled* Da Vinci to create the Mona Lisa.

Similarly, management models all but ignore the learning journey of organisations—the events and circumstances that give each organisation its unique character. While it's obvious to all that a paint-by-numbers Mona Lisa model is but a caricature of the original, this is much less obvious in the case of management models with cool sounding names, hawked by ultra-cool consultancies and big name business school professors. You simply cannot "paint the numbers" and shortcut your way past the learning journey. The sad fact is that most of the models proposed by academics and consultants are *selective* in that they ignore the learning journey and other hard-to-capture aspects of the real world (see Pearce, 2004, Hambrick, 2007, Chia & Holt, 2008, for more examples of such selectivity).

The other side of the coin is what model-makers choose to keep. In general, management models are not based on any one particular case study or reference. They are often the combined result of retrospective examination of many successful organisations. Apart from the fact that such studies are flawed because they only look at successes, not failures, they work towards creating a mythical picture of an ideal organisation. The problem is such an ideal does not exist (no matter what CEOs think).

But as the old saying goes, sex sells. Like catwalk-strutting humans, management models look great and present attractive and highly desirable pictures of what things ought to be. As a result, model makers (and those trying to paint the numbers) are often infatuated with their models and are thus blinded to their flaws.

It goes even further than seduction ... and we now come to a theme we elaborate on in much of this book. Models also serve to reduce anxiety in the sense that they convey a sense of order and security, to meet the all-too-human need to be seen to be doing things the "right" way. For example, many organisations seeking "quality" often end up drowning in an overload of process and documentation that results from focusing on painting the numbers of whichever quality improvement model they have chosen to implement. In reality, little value has been provided. Indeed, one could argue that barriers have been put up because people now have to go through mindless processes, checklists and assessments. But hey, people now feel good because what they are doing *feels right*. Moreover, and this is important too, their rears are covered because they are following a process or model prescribed by their organisation.

Another important aspect of models is the implication that *specified actions or factors will lead to the same outcomes every single time*. This kind of thinking, which has its origins in the natural sciences, is called *causal thinking*. The important fact that management academics and high-end consultants overlook is causal thinking, though fine for physics or engineering, doesn't quite work in the messy world of organisations. The reason for this is pretty obvious when you think about it. Humans, unlike atoms and molecules, do not behave in consistently predictable ways. While one knows that heat applied to water will produce steam at a particular temperature, the same cannot be said for how people will react when the organisational temperature is raised. This is because human actions are driven by intentions (Ghoshal, 2005; Elster, 1989), and intentions cannot be manipulated in the way molecules can. We elaborate on this at length later in this book, and also discuss how intentions can be shifted.

It is important to note that we are not suggesting *causality*[2] be jettisoned. That would be akin to throwing out the proverbial baby with the bathwater (and this book would be shelved under M for Mysticism rather than Management). We think Russell Ackoff (Ackoff & Emery, 2005) is on the right track when he noted that an acorn "causes" (i.e. is necessary for) an oak tree, but an acorn by itself is not enough; one also needs to have the right soil and weather conditions. In other words, one has to consider not just the acorn but also *its environment*.

Why is the environment important? The environment is what determines whether or not the acorn will grow into a healthy oak.

This thinking applies to the world of organisations too. In Chapter 5, we'll tell you the story of Richard Hackman, a Harvard Business School academic who found that as far as team performance is concerned, *conditions trump causes*. Specifically, he found it is far more important for leaders to create the right environment than to get too

---

[2] Causality refers to the relationship between two or more non-synchronous events wherein the last event of the sequence is a consequence of the preceding events. This can sometimes lead to interesting paradoxes like the perennial puzzler about the chicken and egg: http://goo.gl/7rFSLj.

caught up about causal factors such as financial rewards or sending in a coach for a poorly performing team. To be sure, it is impossible to control all aspects of the environment in which an organisation exists. Nevertheless, *every manager has some influence over the environment in which his or her team operates.*

...which lever?

The academics and consultants who propose different management models know (even if they do not say) that their models are incomplete representations of reality. Indeed, the point is that models can represent only selected aspects of reality. So although they may be useful in certain circumstances, they *should never be seen as panaceas.*

The aphorism "All models are wrong, some are useful" (Box, 1979) captures this sentiment perfectly. To use a model wisely, one must *first understand its underlying assumptions and hence, its limitations.* Unfortunately, assumptions are often not made clear because model peddlers want to emphasise the benefits of their models rather than dwell on their limitations (as the truth will likely stop you from using them). In metaphorical terms, the beauty of all models is skin deep; once you get past surface appearances, they are not quite what they seem. Our next example illustrates why models must be subject to a rigorous examination, not just from the perspective of the assumptions that underlie them, but also some very basic validity checks. After all, model-makers are human, and humans, unlike divine beings, are prone to err. Unfortunately, sometimes their errors can have global consequences...

Don't forget to carry the one

When we started working on this book, many countries such as Greece were still dealing with creditor-imposed austerity and its aftermath. Readers will no doubt recall the sense of hopelessness and social unrest that pervaded many of the countries in which fiscal discipline (i.e. deep reduction in government spending) was administered as a *proven* cure for economic ills.

Why were governments so obsessed with controlling debt rather than stimulating growth?

It turns out that a substantial part of the intellectual justification for debt control was based on a highly cited paper by two Harvard University economists (Reinhart & Rogoff, 2010) who claimed *any country that let its government debt rise to over 90% of the GDP would suffer an abrupt, precipitous drop in growth (a very bad thing indeed for an economy)*. Based on their analysis, Reinhart and Rogoff concluded that government debt must be contained at all costs.

This conclusion was music to the ears of many politicians and IMF types because like all neat models, it was simple to understand. More importantly, it appeared to imply a direct cause-effect relationship between high-levels of indebtedness and a drop in growth. Indeed, many politicians took the Reinhart-Rogoff paper to justify their belief that high levels of indebtedness *caused* a drop in growth. Here's what a couple of them said and wrote:

- George Osborne, UK treasurer, once said, *"they [Reinhart and Rogoff] demonstrate convincingly that all financial crises ultimately have their origins in one thing—rapid and unsustainable increases in debt"* (Toynbee, 2013).
- Paul Ryan, Vice Presidential candidate in 2012, wrote, *"Essentially, the [Reinhart Rogoff] study confirmed that the massive debts of the kind the nation is on track to accumulate are associated with stagflation—a toxic mix of economic stagnation and rising inflation"* (Miller & Kowalski, 2013).

At this point, the Reinhart and Rogoff model took on the characteristics of a supermodel, with its elegance and "good looks" being further amplified as the number of citations grew.

Then in April 2013, Thomas Herndon, Michael Ash and Robert Pollin (2013) published a paper describing some basic flaws in the arguments of Reinhart and Rogoff, thereby debunking the alleged extent of the causal connection between debt and growth. In brief, they found the following problems:

- **Data selectivity:** Reinhart and Rogoff inadvertently excluded data for high debt-high growth countries.
- **Non-standard weighting:** Countries with different numbers of data points were weighted identically. Because of the nature of their dataset this (unjustified) weighting favoured high debt-low growth data.
- **Formula error:** This one is truly unbelievable. It turned out the Excel worksheet which they used for their calculations had an error in the formula. Cells that should have been included when calculating an average were not included!

Consider the number of lives that have been turned upside down (if not destroyed altogether) because of the unwavering belief that certain economic decision-makers had in the Reinhart-Rogoff work. Governments made decisions to reduce spending in the belief that it would stimulate growth ... and they bet their citizens' livelihoods on it.

The point is not so much that Reinhart and Rogoff made mistakes (although it has to be said the Excel issue was an absolute clanger). More problematic is the fact that their conclusions appeared to justify a particular belief about the link between indebtedness and growth—a belief that permitted certain ideologically driven decision-makers to do what they did, ignoring all the other factors that go into determining a complex issue like economic growth.

The Reinhart-Rogoff story is a stark reminder that it is critically important to understand the assumptions behind a model, the intention of the model-makers and the context in which those assumptions and intentions are valid. Granted, this involves some effort because it requires a level of enquiry that goes much deeper than quadrants, pillars or forces. Popular models, the kind we have referred to as supermodels, invariably end up being applied to situations where they are wholly inappropriate. Among other things, this implies that those who use a model ought to develop an appreciation of its history, how it came about and what it was originally intended to do. Without such an understanding of history, one is doomed to repeat the mistakes of the past.

Looking back, looking ahead

We are now at the point where, having whetted your appetite, we might be expected to follow the standard textbook model of outlining our key contentions and telling you what we are going to talk about in the ensuing chapters. While we could do that, our proposition is to let our story unfold as all good stories should. Rich conversations are never linear; they are varied and often contain unexpected surprises—and we'd like to think of this book as such a conversation between you the reader and us.

What we will say at this early point is this: the tagline of this book, "the art of harnessing ambiguity" is what we want to get to eventually and this is best done in an indirect way. So rather than define ambiguity and its implications up front, we are going to arrive at it.

In the next chapter, we take a potted history of a century of management thought, to see just how much we actually have progressed. Following that … well, you are just going to have to read on and accept the ambiguity of not having the path laid out for you!

(…and we did warn you in the opening paragraph that you'd be asked to "go with it"!)

2

The Unbearable Inconsistency of Management Knowledge

"On the surface, an intelligible lie; underneath, the unintelligible truth."

—Milan Kundera, The Unbearable Lightness of Being

Edwin's story

When Edwin joined the company, he inherited a team disdained by the business for their inefficiency and lack of results. There was no doubt in his own mind that he would fix it; he had to, given he was hired to bring "fresh thinking" into an organisation that was feeling the bite of industry disruption. Their business model that had worked for more than half a century was fraying at the edges, if not quite falling apart.

In a fit of we-must-do-something-soon, management took the standard route prescribed by Big Q consultants: cost cutting and consolidation of services in the name of achieving efficiency. Edwin had done multiple stints with big name tech firms, known for their focus on so-called scientific, metric-driven methods of employee management. Given the new direction of the organisation, he was an ideal choice for a frontline manager role.

In something reminiscent of a shock and awe campaign, Edwin made it abundantly clear that much greater efficiency was required. He pressured his inherited team hard from the get go. They worked extraordinarily long hours, yet were constantly berated for not doing more. If mistakes were made, they were publicly aired and the unfortunates who made them ridiculed. Employees who Edwin perceived as being low-performers were put under extra pressure with the intent of making them leave.

His peers, most of whom had been with the organisation a long time, watched on in appalled fascination. What would be the result of all this, they wondered. Surely, he could not get away with treating his people like machines.

But Edwin knew what he was doing; the results were exactly what he said they'd be:

- The team, for the first time in history, started delivering projects on time and within budget.
- In addition to their regular project work, the team bid for work in other regions, got it, and delivered as promised.

- Edwin started to get more funding. Indeed, because of his exemplary delivery record, he was the only manager in the regional office who was able to get funding for multi-million dollar projects.

The take home lesson for Edwin's peers seemed to be that the ends justified the means.

Things went on in this vein for a year or two. Edwin's stock rose steadily; he was seen as an up and coming star. Were it not for his prickly personality which had rubbed a number of his peers the wrong way, he would surely have been given an opportunity to move to corporate on promotion.

Rumblings of discontent from Edwin's team occasionally found their way to corporate. When queried, he dismissed these as the last gasp of an underperforming minority. Corporate managers were only too happy to buy this line. They needed Edwin because he made them look good too.

Sure, some people left, but Edwin's modus operandi was clever and devious. Over many months, he would assign employees who were on his hit list to projects he knew they would not be able to handle. When the inevitable occurred, he would publicise their failures, which created the perception that the said employees were incompetent. To create an illusion of fairness, he would then give them more "chances" of this nature with similar results, thus guaranteeing their voluntary or involuntary departure.

It worked a treat: one employee was managed out, another left because of the stress, yet another got a job elsewhere. Edwin hired a senior person to replace one of the employees but did not fill the other two positions. Unfortunately, the new guy lasted about six months; he couldn't handle the toxic work environment.

Now losing one team member can be attributed to bad luck, and losing two may be explained away by a favourable job market. Losing three, however, starts to ring alarm bells in HR and losing four confirms their fears, especially if the fourth is the person who replaced the first.

All of a sudden Edwin became a focus of attention from corporate. He was too valuable to lose of course, results still trumped all else.

However, he was assigned a coach and informed that employee retention would be one of his KPIs henceforth.

This caused a remarkable turnaround in Edwin's attitude. Instead of talking about processes and compliance, he spoke of people and collaboration. The rhetoric of stack rankings, KPIs and targets were replaced by that of organisational culture and employee engagement ratings. Models like the Jack Welch Vitality Curve were supplanted by others akin to Kotter's 8 Step Process for Leading Change. Incentives were given away like there was no tomorrow, and team-building events to raise morale became regular slots in the team calendar. Most importantly, he hired more contract staff to ease the workload on struggling but high value internal staff.

The measures seemed to work. People seemed genuinely happier and morale improved.

The changes wrought by Edwin cost money of course. Fortunately, he had enough of it from all the project funding he had garnered for that year. Deep down, he knew he would not be able to sustain the changes unless he managed to secure higher levels of funding in the following years. As the year wound down though, industry disruption was hitting even harder, and it became clear this might not happen.

Faced with the possibility of a shrinking budget and his reputation at risk, you can probably guess how Edwin's behaviour changed (yet again!). The people on his team were not surprised by what they saw as Edwin's reversion to type.

As one of the survivors on his team noted pithily, "You can polish a turd all day but it remains a turd."

Individual and collective schizophrenia

In academia, you know you are on a path to stardom when your citation count (the number of times your paper is cited) is high. The logic here is simple: the greater the number of citations, the greater the impact of ideas presented in the paper.

To that end, Stephen Barley and Gideon Kunda scored an academic hit with their 1992 paper entitled, "Design and Devotion: Surges of

Rational and Normative Ideologies of Control in Managerial Discourse" (Barley & Kunda, 1992). Despite its tedious and undecipherable title, the paper has been widely cited: 1371 citations according to Google Scholar as we write this. We speculate its popularity is due to the fact that it sheds light on the somewhat schizophrenic behaviour of our friend Edwin.

Most management models and fashions seem to be derived from two broad managerial styles that can be characterised as *process-oriented* or *people-oriented.* The first takes its inspiration from the hard sciences (such as physics) whereas the second is rooted in the social sciences (such as psychology and sociology). Although both ultimately aim at control, they achieve it in very different ways. This is reflected in the different models favoured by each managerial style. Of course, no manager is totally process or people-oriented, but just like Edwin, most show an affinity for one style over the other—the preferred style being the one they revert to under stress.

It is easy to presume that management has evolved in a logical manner, progressing along a "wisdom continuum" from process-dominated to people-focused approaches. Such a progression seems to make intuitive sense, especially in view of the recent rise of knowledge-based industries as opposed to the process-oriented manufacturing industries of the early 20th century. Barley and Kunda, however, claim that such a progression is a myth. Analysing the history of management thought over the last century and half, they concluded that *the dominant ideology switches every two to three decades from a process-oriented approach to a people-oriented one and vice versa.* Each approach holds sway for a generation or two, before dissatisfaction and/or changing economic conditions drive a reversal of momentum in the other direction, much like the oscillatory motion of a seesaw as shown in Figure 2.1.

Thus it appears the schizophrenic behaviour exhibited by stressed managers such as Edwin is displayed by the discipline of management as a whole, but across generational timeframes! This begs the obvious question of why? Can't people simply merge the best elements of both styles or better yet, switch from one to the other at will?

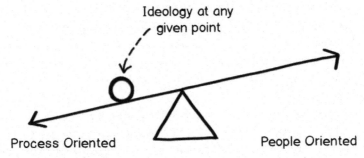

Figure 2.1: The oscillation between process and people oriented management ideology

This is a very good question which we will fully address in Chapter 3, but for now, let's look at an important consequence of this collective schizophrenia—a remarkable tendency to forget the lessons of the past.

"That's only 10%…"

One of Paul's former colleagues, Darryl Whiteley, who is mentioned in our previous book (Culmsee & Awati, 2013) is a veteran project manager in the construction and engineering industry. He has been in the field for close to forty years, is a fellow of the Institute of Engineers and has marked exams at the local university for those studying a Master's Degree in Project Management. In short, Darryl knows his stuff.

During a conversation some years ago, Darryl was talking about his work in utilising highly collaborative approaches to project delivery in the traditionally confrontational construction industry. He mentioned that such collaborative approaches entailed the application of *good project management practice*. Paul knew what Darryl meant by this statement, but commented that some people might equate a statement like "good project management practice" to things such as a well-developed Gantt chart listing activities with names, tasks and times (Gantt charts are the quintessential project management supermodel).

Darryl's reply was dismissive. "At best that's only 1/10th of what project management is really about," he said, lamenting that those who criticise traditional project management are actually criticising a small subset of the discipline. For him, their criticisms are based on an incomplete view of what the discipline is all about. Unsurprisingly, their "solutions" are misinformed or address a problem that has already been solved … and they would see this if only they took the time and trouble to do so.

This is a common pattern that is particularly noticeable in our modern era of connectivity, social networking and distributed communities of practice. Crusaders of a particular methodology, framework, model or practice will waste no time dumping on whatever they have grown to dislike, and will swear that their "new approach" addresses the gaps. They often push the seesaw the other way to right such wrongs, while those on the other side do all they can to keep the seesaw where it is, arguing that the crusaders aren't really inventing anything new, and that if a gap exists at all, it is in the critics' knowledge of the domain they are taking to task.

Similarly, another colleague of Paul's who was mentioned in the last book, Mike Kapitola, told him a story about the first Total Quality Management (TQM) workshop he attended in the late 1980s. While Mike was inspired and excited by the content, an old-timer in the room was less enthused, grumbling that it was just Operations and Methods (O&M) with a new coat of paint. Mike dismissed this criticism as typical of a change-resistant curmudgeon and proceeded to immerse himself in the brave new world of TQM. Fast forward many years of hard earned experience, Mike found himself in a workshop where Six Sigma was being touted as the means to "finally get organised". Many in the room were inspired and excited, but Mike's reaction was "this is just TQM reinvented." A split second later he realised he was now the old timer. In a more recent reflection on this story, Mike said:

> "I see it now as youthful enthusiasm in discovering something for the first time that has been around for generations, just under a new name. In reality, good principles endure over time and are incorporated into the next fad. The challenge is to know and understand what is happening without growing old and cynical. Wisdom

and perspective sometimes comes with age and experience, but sometimes we just get old!" (personal communication, Feb 8, 2016).

From project management to systems thinking…

Paul saw this same pattern some time later when he joined a Design Thinking discussion group on LinkedIn[3]. He'd read about Design Thinking during its hype phase a few years earlier, and on reading more up to date literature on the topic, instinctively thought, "Isn't a lot of this just Systems Thinking[4] reinvented?"

The reason for this is Paul had always identified himself as a reasonably pragmatic systems thinker (we say pragmatic because although systems thinkers will not like us saying so, many are armchair critics and philosophers). Paul is a user of many systems thinking-based tools and approaches so he was naturally curious to understand how design thinkers see themselves as different from systems thinkers.

To do this, he followed several very long discussion threads on a LinkedIn group where the question had been raised. Unfortunately, none of the explanations seemed clear or convincing and no one had really nailed the difference between the two disciplines. Eventually he turned from LinkedIn forums to the literature and finally found a paper which went into some detail on the two disciplines and offered some distinctions between them (Pourdehnad, Wilson, & Wexler, 2011). We won't bother you with the content, except to say it was a good read which left Paul with the following choices about his understanding of Systems and Design Thinking:

- Option 1: His understanding of Systems Thinking was wrong and he was in fact a design thinker all along

---

[3] https://www.linkedin.com/groups/37821/profile
[4] http://en.wikipedia.org/wiki/Systems_thinking

- Option 2: He was indeed a systems thinker and a lot of Design Thinking is Systems Thinking with a pragmatic bent

It has to be said that if it takes academic research to work out the difference between two ideologies, then one has to wonder if there is much of a difference for a lay person or even a professional. But such musings are unnecessary nowadays as both were supplanted by Stoos ... well, according to Stoosians anyway.

From #systemsthinking to #stoos

In early 2012, the Stoos Movement[5] emerged from the work of a group of individuals from different disciplines and countries who came together in Stoos, Switzerland, to discuss problems they perceived in existing management structures and paradigms. No doubt, participating in the event would have been an exhilarating and inspiring experience—a bunch of diverse people bringing their perspectives and experiences together to develop new understandings of organisations and how they ought to be run. How could it not have been fun? Of course, it is impossible to translate into words the experience of actually being there. Indeed, it is when one tries to codify such tacit experiences that their similarities to what has come before become apparent.

Both of us had become aware of the Stoos Movement via Twitter, and we followed it via the #stoos hashtag. To put our interest in context, we had at that time just launched the first edition of our previous book in which we had discussed how nascent ideas and movements gain legitimacy in the professional world[6]. We followed the early evolution of the #stoos movement because it was a perfect example of a movement in the making. After reading the Stoos website, tweets, blogs and videos, we felt a sense of déjà vu. A good bit of the writing by Stoos thought leaders bore an uncanny similarity to what design thinkers had written in years past.

---

[5] http://www.stoosnetwork.org/
[6] See Chapter 3 of (Culmsee & Awati, 2013)

Paul wryly commented to Kailash, "I bet someone will eventually complain that this is just Design Thinking reinvented."

Guess what ... a short time later that's exactly what happened. Someone posted that very assertion on Twitter! We speculate this person may have been a design thinker who felt the Stoosians were merely reinventing a wheel they painstakingly constructed. We were tempted to remark that systems thinkers could make a similar claim vis-à-vis Design Thinking ... but then we realised that there's quite likely a precursor to Systems Thinking that the two of us were not aware of.

Unfortunately for the Stoos crowd, they did not achieve the necessary critical mass to gain mindshare and momentum, and hence are not particularly active as we write this.

The decay (and remarkable recurrence) of knowledge...

The aforementioned stories illustrate a pattern of great enthusiasm combined with a lack of awareness, narrow focus or plain misinterpretation of what has come before. As a result, it seems there is a natural human tendency to reinvent the wheel, slap a new label on and tout it as the best thing since the invention of sliced bread. One cannot but help wonder if any "new" ideas or movements are *truly* new.

Any corpus of knowledge is a bunch of memes: ideas, behaviours or styles that spread from person to person within a culture[7]. Indeed, entire disciplines such as project management can be viewed as a bunch of memes that have been codified into a body of knowledge (Whitty, 2005). Some memes are "sticky" in that they are more readily retained and communicated, while others seem less able to get traction and mindshare.

Similarly, a person indoctrinated in a standard business school curriculum inevitably sees real-life situations through the lens of the models (or memes!) he or she is familiar with. To paraphrase a well-known saying: if one is familiar only with a hammer, every problem

---

[7] http://en.wikipedia.org/wiki/Meme

appears to be a nail. Sometimes the wielder of the metaphorical hammer may realise that not all problems yield to hammering. In other words, the models they have been using are incomplete, or even incorrect. They then cast about for something that will work better. In the present day world, one doesn't have to search too far because there are several convenient corpuses of knowledge to choose from, each one with a ready supply of models that allegedly make more sense than the ones that came before ... and as an added bonus, many of them offer certifications to prove to the world at large that one has mastered them.

However, the fact that fads come and go, and like Stoos, rarely linger (unless of course, you follow our patented instructions in Chapter 1), suggests something is missing. Some aspects of reality can truly be grasped only through experience, not models. It is experience that highlights the difference between the real-world and the simplistic one that is captured in models. Reality consists of complex, messy situations, so any attempt to capture it through concepts and models will necessarily be incomplete. In the light of this, it is easy to see why old knowledge is continually rediscovered, albeit in a different form. Since models attempt to grasp the ungraspable, they will all contain many similarities but will also have some differences. Systems Thinking, Design Thinking and the Stoos Movement, are rooted in the same reality, so their similarities should not be surprising.

It seems those who come up with new labels to reflect their new understandings are paradoxically both wise and narrow-minded at the same time. They are wise in that they seek better models to understand the reality they encounter, but at the same time they are narrow-minded because they are likely glossing over or trashing some worthwhile ones too. Reality is multifaceted and cannot be captured in any one model.

The bottom line here is that the finders of new truths should take care they do not get carried away by their own hyperbole.

The cost of forgetting

It is a truism that those who do not learn from history are condemned to repeat it. In the cases we have just illustrated, this forgetting and reinventing is essentially harmless because all we have to put up with is a bunch of earnest flag-wavers who keep proclaiming that they have invented something profound. It is possible to ignore them, and indeed that is what most of us do.

However, there is a darker side of the decay and recurrence (or decline and resurrection) of management models: it increases the likelihood of neglecting the things that really matter, only to rediscover them by painfully relearning the lessons of the past. To explain why, we are going to have to go back more than a century in time...

Frederick Winslow Taylor, if you have not come across him before, was a hugely influential management thinker, regarded by many as the first modern management guru. In common with many management gurus, he is also a highly polarizing figure who is seen either as a misunderstood visionary or the root of all management evil. His claim to fame is that he is the father of *Scientific Management*—a management approach that aimed to bring a degree of quantitative, scientific rigour to the world of work. Taylor's ideas, which really took off in the early part of the 20th century, were aimed at replacing gut-feel and rule-of-thumb based management approaches with optimised work processes based on measurement and standardisation.

Sounds good so far, right? Indeed, the rhetoric here sounds no different to what is often heard in the boardrooms and meeting rooms of today's organisations.

Taylor was a staunch believer in the power of science to unambiguously determine the most optimal work processes. He stated this point of view quite clearly in the introduction to his bestseller, *The Principles of Scientific Management* (Taylor F. W., 1911):

> "This paper has been written ... to prove that the best management is a true science, resting upon clearly defined laws, rules and principles, as a foundation. And further to show that the fundamental principles of scientific management are applicable to all human activities, from our simplest individual activities to the work of great corporations, which call for the most elaborate cooperation. And briefly, through a series of

illustrations, to convince the reader that whenever these principles are correctly applied, results must follow which are truly astounding…" (p. 7).

There are two obvious claims in these lines. The first is that such laws exist and can be found. The second is that the application of these laws will lead to truly outstanding results—subject of course to you applying them correctly. But a careful reading of Taylor's book reveals he claimed much more. Indeed, he asserted that workers would love these methods. Why? Because as part of redesigning work practices, bonuses were paid to those who exceeded performance targets. If measurements showed some workers were not as productive as they ought to be, they could be redeployed to tasks better suited to their capabilities, thus giving them a better chance to get bonuses too. Accordingly, he reasoned that even the least-skilled worker would recognize the superiority of rationally optimised work. In Taylor's words:

"…scientific rules would be immensely helpful for them in achieving a full realisation of their capabilities and a maximisation of their earning potential" (p. 36).

At this point you might be thinking, "that sounds a bit like my workplace." After all, today's organisations are big on measurement, streamlined process, integrated reporting and job optimisation with an army of consultants lurking in the corridors. Some things never change: back in the 1900s there was also an army of consultants, but they were armed with stopwatches, not iPads.

Barley & Kunda (1992) asserted that the following three assumptions underpinned scientific management:

1. An unshakable belief in the utility and morality of scientific reasoning,
2. The belief that all people are primarily rational and will change their behaviours and approaches if a new practice demonstrated clear advantage, and

3. The belief that all people view work as an economic endeavour (in other words, pay is the single factor that motivates us to work).

Now reading these assumptions, you might think "hmm ... that does not sound like my workplace," and we would agree. All these premises are indeed questionable ... and we all know that logic gets you nowhere if your premise is wrong. So although scientific management gained a lot of management mindshare (which ensured Taylor and his acolytes became high-end consultants), several widely publicised and respected government studies in the 1920s cast doubt on Tayloristic claims of having achieved "outstanding results".

The demise of Taylorism

What happened? Why did the promise of the perpetually well-oiled machine-like organisation never eventuate? We have briefly mentioned some of the reasons in the previous section. Here's a more complete picture that draws upon the work of Fleischman (2000).

In short, Taylor was extremely naïve about workers' reactions to his methods. As it turned out, *many of them hated the new approach*. This was not helped by the fact that Taylor deemed most of them were not *"capable of fully understanding the science involved"* (Taylor F. W., 1911, p. 26). He therefore implemented all process changes in a top-down manner in which workers were directed by stopwatch wielding consultants. We're sure you can understand how well that went down with the workers.

Taylor was also naïve about what motivated workers. His methods tended to fragment work into small chunks with each worker being assigned their "chunk". As a result, individuals felt devalued: they were no more than small cogs in a big machine and were being de-skilled by being forced to focus on highly specific functions.

At a collective level, unions also were resistant to the changes. The very notion of individual bonuses and incentives went against the principles of collective bargaining. As a result, relations between unions and Taylorists became increasingly adversarial.

If that wasn't enough, Taylor ran into problems with factory owners and entrepreneurs too! Since they were the ones shelling out cash, they expected good returns on their investment in reasonable timeframes. However, implementing Taylor's approach required a small army of managers, administrators and consultants for extended periods of time. In 1903, Taylor stated that twice the number of foremen would be required during the introduction of the new system (Taylor, 1903, p. 129). Apart from the inevitable managerial-level politics that ensued, the workers were burdened by serving more masters than ever before.

Taylor was also insistent that the groundwork had to be carefully laid for his system to work, and that it might take two to five or more years to implement scientific management "properly". He also warned about the mindset needed and the dangers of piecemeal adoption:

> "When, however, the elements of this mechanism ... are being used without being accompanied by the true philosophy of [scientific] management, the results are in many cases disastrous. And, unfortunately, even when men who are thoroughly in sympathy with the principles of scientific management undertake to change too rapidly from the old type to the new, without heeding the warnings of those who have had years of experience in making this change, they frequently meet with serious troubles, and sometimes with strikes, followed by failure" (Taylor, 1911, p. 130).

In modern terms, one can interpret that quote as a warning to implementers not to "paint by numbers". But in the end it didn't matter. Taylor died in 1915 and by the mid-1920s his ideology was on the outer edges of management thought, having been displaced by newer ideas. However, his rhetoric of "if it fails, it is your fault for not doing it right" remains the refuge of best-practices apologists to this day.

So much for Taylor and scientific management ... allegedly.

Meanwhile in Japan...

After Taylorism had its day, the seesaw of Figure 2.1 swung the other way for a generation, with "human relations" moving to centre stage in management thinking. This term came to encompass all the things that would now be known as collaboration and collective intelligence. With this movement, the rationalism of scientific management gave way to a human-centric view of workers as social beings driven by needs such as a sense of belonging and competence. Teamwork and workplace harmony received a lot of focus, and management theorists started to make fine distinctions between *leadership* and *management,* with the latter taking on a somewhat pejorative tone. Desirable competencies went from technical skills like operating stop-watches and the ability to do statistical calculations, to so-called soft skills that encompass things such as communication and understanding group dynamics.

By the mid-1950s, this end of the ideological seesaw bumped up against its own built-in limitations. The price paid for cohesion and loyalty was the loss of individualism and a "homogenizing mediocrity" (Barley & Kunda, 1992). Firms became cumbersome and slow to respond to change. This became especially apparent when economic conditions forced organisations to tackle new challenges that required creative thought and independent behaviours from employees.

Meanwhile though, in faraway post-war Japan, companies applied the *apparently* discredited "rational" principles of Taylor in a way that would eventually enable them to outperform US companies.

Wait ... does that mean Taylorism worked after all?

To truly answer that question, we would have to retell the entire, highly nuanced history of 20th century management (and as you will soon see, a lot of it is more myth than fact). What we will say is this: it is absolutely true that a lot of the tools and principles devised by Taylor and his acolytes did work *under Japanese conditions.* However, as we will see, the truth about what these conditions are is somewhat contentious, even to this day!

In an irony of history, the Japanese methods (which originated in the US) were exported back to the US in the guise of frameworks such as

Total Quality Management (TQM) and later, Lean Manufacturing. Driven by "Japan envy" (we need to work like the Japanese do), Western organisations first took to TQM in the 1980s with the unbridled enthusiasm of those who have seen the light for the first time. TQM became a new management supermodel, complete with its evangelical army of consultants who were more than happy to help organisations implement it … "properly" of course.

Coincidentally, while this was happening, the management ideology seesaw of Figure 2.1 had tilted back to the human-centric side. This meant the focus was not just the tools of TQM and Lean, but considerable attention was given to organisational climates and cultures as well. This fostered a plethora of business books that, to this day, influence senior management who initiate excruciating programs to develop these "desirable cultures". Employees were sent off to culture seminars and mission, vision and value statements adorned the walls of corporate reception areas and meeting rooms. Quality was touted as the end product of a *state of mind* that required a revolution in the way both managers and workers understood their roles.

Hmm … you see the pattern here, right? The story hereon is so predictable that it is farcical.[8]

Unfortunately for many organisations, TQM did not live up to their lofty expectations. Moreover, like scientific management eighty years' earlier, it cost a lot of money too. As this is more recent history, the failures of TQM are better documented than those from Taylor's time. For example, Harari (1997) claimed that only about one-fifth, or at best one-third, of the TQM programs in the US and Europe had achieved any tangible improvements in quality, productivity, competitiveness or financial results at all.

How could this be? How could organisations that take into account *both process and human centric viewpoints*, fail to successfully implement TQM?

While we could explore the answer to that question now, it doesn't matter that much because by the early 1990s, TQM was quickly

---

[8] Karl Marx once said that history repeats itself, first as tragedy then as farce

forgotten and Lean became all the rage. So we'll save the answer for the next chapter and first take a look at how Lean fared...

Leaning to Taylor again

Both TQM and Lean had their origins in a manufacturing system developed in the 1950s at Toyota called the Toyota Production System (Ohno, 1988). TPS, which has come to be revered outside of Japan, was directly influenced by Taylor and his successors. It focused on the eminently Tayloristic concern of eliminating waste—whether it be in time, materials or money—to improve efficiency.

The reasons why Taylorist ideas worked better in Japan are much more nuanced than the official story which posits that Japanese corporate culture creates a family-like work environment that values long-term thinking, respect for and direct involvement of workers, and the responsibility of leaders to be teachers and trainers. This paints the picture that workers were not mere cogs in a giant industrial machine and therefore this was not the same as the bad old days of Taylorism. Quoting from Krafcik (1988), who coined the term "Lean Production":

> "Management did not think of workers as replaceable cogs in a great production machine ... and gave them the responsibility to continuously improve ... Scientific management techniques were not thrown away; they were just performed by different, more appropriate employees" who had a "true grass-roots involved with all aspects of the operation" (p. 43).

This explanation has been offered for many years and has become folklore. Indeed, it is the basis for the "people first" principles that pervade what practitioners now call "Lean thinking". However, various insiders have questioned the official story, the main contention being the western sense of teamwork is not the same as the Japanese sense (Dankbaar, 1997) and that *TPS in reality has little resemblance to the way it is packaged and presented to the west* (Pruijt, 2003). Darius Mehri, who lived in

Japan and worked within the TPS regime wrote a stinging critique in 2006 and in his subsequent book, said:

> "I came to view the lauded TPS system with a certain level of skepticism; with first-hand knowledge and first-person accounts of the impact the system has on worker safety, stress, creativity and innovation, overtime, and low morale, I came to question the assumed value of its rigors. TPS had achieved high productivity, yes. Toyota maintains a powerful global market share, yes. Their product development process is relentless at achieving continual improvement, certainly. But at what price?" (Mehri, 2006, p. 22).

In relation to attitudes to teamwork, Mehri described teams operating more as rigidly defined groups of individuals, with team members taking direction from their manager and working independently of other team members *without much consultation or collaboration.* Furthermore, information was not free-flowing. Non-managerial engineers focused solely on their small part in the whole, and the comprehensive sense of how all of the parts work together lay only with the managers. Here is how he put it:

> "Often, when Western scholars describe teamwork, they infer that all Japanese engineers—even lower level engineers—share information and collaborate. However, this is simply not true. All information and work was controlled from above. Even in the lunchroom, there was no open talk about technology or sharing of ideas" (p. 31).

Whether you agree with Mehri's insider critique or not, the point is that if you discount the underlying principles the Japanese purportedly used in relation to worker involvement, there is little difference between TPS and Taylorism. Why? Because all that remains is a hair splitting discussion on what tools were used, and for what purpose. Such a discussion, while very common, totally misses the point because *tools have little to do with the success (or failure) of the methods*. This foreshadows a point we will dwell on at length later—that *conditions* are more important than tools.

The point we want you to take away for now is that the key factor cited as being responsible for the differences between the "bad old days" of Taylorism and newfound wisdom of Lean Thinking (i.e. respect for humanity, involvement of workers and a bottom up view of management) is questionable. It is a romanticised view of the reality of life under TPS, which by some accounts, appears very cog-like and Tayloristic indeed. In fact, some authors have claimed that Lean is Taylorism perfected. For example, a recent examination of Lean (McCann, Hassard, Granter, & Hyde, 2015) stated:

> "Examples of lean as 'perfected Taylorism' are provided by Japanese (e.g. Kamata, 1983; Mouer and Kawanishi, 2005; Tamura, 2006) and UK/US authors (e.g. Carter et al., 2011; Delbridge, 1998; Graham, 1995; Stewart et al., 2009), and indeed many Toyota-affiliated engineers openly emphasize the consistency of TPS with Taylorism (Coffey, 2006)" (p. 1560 - see original text for references).

What this means is Lean cannot lay claim to have introduced the "breakthrough idea" of bottom up management, worker involvement and inclusion. Indeed, the claim simply echoes our point that good principles tend to be rediscovered time and again.

Lean rebooted

The concept of Lean has subsequently expanded into industries and sectors far removed from its manufacturing roots. For example, it has been applied in service industries like healthcare and fast-moving companies such as Silicon Valley start-ups. In relation to the latter, the concept of *Lean Startup* emerged around the late 2000's (Ries, 2011).

Lean Startup is essentially an attempt to use Lean principles (as well as Design Thinking and other ideas) to help small new companies build innovative new products "under conditions of extreme uncertainty". This is done via "validated learning"—an approach in which *all* assumptions are empirically tested via experimentation and measurement. Essentially, if you cannot *prove* an assumption about your product, business model or customer behaviours with quantifiable evidence, you are not practicing Lean Startup and are probably wasting time and money.

Startups are ideal for the application of Lean principles because they generally have highly motivated teams, bottom-up management structures and perhaps most critically, an extreme paucity of resources. When funds are non-existent, any incorrect assumptions regarding product development could turn out to be fatal.

As we write this, elements of Lean Startup have become popular outside of its Silicon Valley origins and many organisations are now adopting them. Perhaps unsurprisingly, key aspects of Lean Startup have been decontextualised and misapplied at large.

The primary concern of the Lean Startup approach is to build a viable product (one that customers would want to buy) and a business model capable of delivering it in the most cost and time efficient way. This is the so-called *minimum viable product*. It is easy to see that the notion of a minimally viable product has all the attributes of a management supermodel. It is simple to explain, memorable and has all the necessary management hooks (Reduce Waste! Lower Costs! Innovate Faster! Improve Efficiency!). No surprise then, that many organisations have adopted it in a quest to be "agile and responsive" to their customers and competition. However, these organisations, which are generally *not* small startups, tend to overlook critical contextual aspects such as team motivation, inclusive management as well as procedural aspects such as validated learning via a relentless focus on measurement.

This reprises the problem we outlined in Chapter 1 where we stated that to use a model wisely, one must *first understand the assumptions that underlie it and hence, its limitations*. A typical startup involves a few visionaries risking all for the glory of bringing their ideas to the masses and (possibly) becoming rich along the way. They have few resources, non-existent processes and are saddled with huge levels of uncertainty. It is difficult for those who have worked solely in established organisations to truly understand what it means to work in such an environment. As a result, when exposed to Lean Startup case studies, they tend to see the models and miss everything else … a tendency that is reflected in oft-asked uninformed questions like "Have you done your MVP yet?" and "Have you pivoted?"

As Darryl might have said, "What they see is at best a tenth of what it is all about."

The (D)evolution of Lean?

Further muddying the waters of today, the seesaw of management ideology is tilting back toward the rationalist, scientific end. This appears to be driven in part by the Internet powered effects of globalisation on how work is organised and overseen, facilitated by real-time surveillance and analytical techniques.

We are now measuring and analysing more than ever before and are entering a world of online marketplaces, not just for Taxis (Uber) and accommodation (AirBnB), but also for less tangible services such as skills. Organisations such as Upwork[9] now provide a marketplace where buyers and sellers can offer and bid for specified human services. If you have not seen it, think of it as eBay for contractors. In such technology-powered marketplaces, the division of labour takes on a whole new meaning. Not only does it transcend geographical and cultural boundaries, it also changes the meaning of work by enabling its break up into ever-finer fragments. An article in the Economist (2015) called this *Digital Taylorism* and suggested it is set to be a more powerful force than its analogue predecessor:

> "Technology allows the division of labour to be applied to a much wider range of jobs: companies such as Upwork are making a business out of slicing clerical

---

[9] https://www.upwork.com/

work into routine tasks and then outsourcing them to
freelancers … The most basic axiom of management is
'what gets measured gets managed'. So the more the
technology of measurement advances, the more we hand
power to Frederick Taylor's successors."

Perhaps Taylorism is the inevitable by-product of global competition
and technology innovation. Perhaps the "cogs in the machine" concerns
are misplaced in this day and age of digitalisation. In truth, the question
of whether or not these Tayloristic trends and the variants of Lean will
be eventually seen as fads will only be settled in the fullness of time. That
said, we strongly recommend that you keep in mind the lesson from
Taylor's experience a century ago: logic not only gets you nowhere if
your premise is wrong, but the erroneous conclusions reached can be
highly costly as well, a point that is well illustrated by the radical changes
in the nature of white collar work.

We have another recommendation too, one that is more in keeping
with the message of this book. If you are reading this book in the far
future where Lean is regarded as a long forgotten and thoroughly
debunked fad, supplanted by something else making big promises, a
"management fad radar" might be just what you need. We will therefore
round out this chapter with such a tool for precisely this job.

The ubiquity of fads

A management fad is a behaviour, technique or method that is
enthusiastically used for a short period of time. We think the short life of
a fad can be attributed to the fact that it is essentially a dodgy model that
sounds plausible, its dodginess becoming evident soon after one starts to
use it. In Kundera's words (re the epigram at the start of the chapter) it is
an intelligible lie.

It is easy to understand why fads catch on easily amongst managers.
Professional management is predicated on the existence of a set of
universal, generic concepts (laws) that underpin management practice
everywhere and at all times. Such presumed universality tends to

diminish the legitimacy of individual experience-based management wisdom (sometimes called gut feel), while enhancing the appeal of pre-packaged techniques.

The life cycle of fads follows a familiar pattern, outlined brilliantly and ironically by Birnbaum's (2000) five-stage model (ironic because we are using models to explain why other models catch on and cause damage!). In keeping with our steps in Chapter 1, we've re-cast it as "Birnbaum (and Culmsee/Awati) "Five Stages of Bullshit Legitimation" and have opted to use the "Cyclique" look as shown in Figure 2.2. We haven't yet worked out a plausible backstory that would make it good management folklore … but given time, we will.

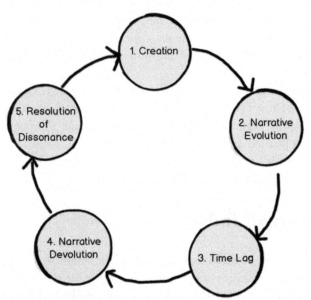

Figure 2.2: Birnbaum (and Culmsee/ Awati) Five Stages of Bullshit Legitimation Model

Here are Birnbaum's stages in detail:

- **Stage 1: Creation:** A new management concept is claimed to be *the* solution to a major problem or to topical challenges.

Consultants push the new concept hard, claiming it to be proven ("this is definitely the real-deal!") and that early adopters have achieved outstanding results.

- **Stage 2: Narrative Evolution:** The fad catches on. It rapidly spreads to high-profile organisations and communities of practice form around it. It is presented as easy to adopt and detractors are labelled as laggards who are change resistant and stalwarts of "old thinking".

- **Stage 3: Time Lag:** The period before user reactions and independent analyses of the fad emerge. Cautionary anecdotes begin to emerge and the rate of adoption slows.

- **Stage 4: Narrative Devolution:** The period where tales of caution give rise to outright scepticism. At this point, the number of detractors grow to a point where the fad is labelled "a fad".

- **Stage 5: Resolution of Dissonance:** The period where evangelists, taking a cue from Taylor, account for the failure of their fad by claiming that implementers are "not doing it properly," rather than considering the possibility that the fad may really be flawed. If pressure persists, they will recycle it after minor modifications, thus launching the Creation stage anew.

It is our contention that most management fads currently in vogue can be placed somewhere on this cycle. Moreover, if you take a clear-eyed view of the history of the fad (as we have attempted to do with Taylorism and its descendants) you will likely find that the five stage model describes its evolution and eventual fate quite accurately.

Like all tools, this model is something of a double-edged sword. It serves as a decent bullshit detector but should you choose to use it for nefarious purposes, it also provides you with a strategy to ensure that your management model remains in vogue. To do the latter, simply follow our instructions in Chapter 1 to create your supermodel, and once reality starts to show up the flaws in your flawless masterpiece, introduce minor caveats or modifications (Stage 5) and create another beautiful model (Stage 1), thereby ensuring your creation stays forever young and attractive.

Conclusion

Our aim in this chapter was to highlight the cyclical nature of management, both at the level of the individual and that of the discipline. Working managers tend to switch between process and people oriented management styles approaches depending on the nature of problems they face, and the discipline as a whole, mirrors this by oscillating between the same two opposing ideologies depending on the economic zeitgeist.

On a related note, we'd like to point out that the coexistence of opposites is not at all a rare occurrence in the world of organisations. One can see a similar oscillation between opposites play out in other areas, an example being the tendency of multinational corporations to swing from decentralisation (autonomous subsidiaries) to centralisation (tight control from corporate), or in the world of IT where the pendulum swings from a focus on technology as a cost of doing business to technology as a source of innovation.

Finally, our tracing of the history of Taylorism from the metal foundries of Pennsylvania at the turn of last century to the present day digital foundries of Silicon Valley shows that even approaches superficially appearing to be of a single type (process-driven in the case of Taylorism) are in reality much more nuanced. Indeed, the secret of success in management seems to hinge on the ability of managers (if not the entire discipline!) to reconcile opposites. However, as we will find out in the next couple of chapters, this is much more easily said than done ... and the reasons for this are far from obvious.

3

Seesaws and Fetishes

Lisa Simpson: [to Homer] By your logic I could claim that this rock keeps tigers away.
Homer Simpson: Oh, how does it work?
Lisa Simpson: It doesn't work.
Homer Simpson: Uh huh.
Lisa Simpson: It's just a stupid rock.
Homer Simpson: Uh huh.
Lisa Simpson: But I don't see any tigers around, do you?
Homer Simpson: Lisa, I want to buy your rock.

The "Fat Kid on a Seesaw" Model of Problem Solving

The notion of left brain versus right brain has been around for years and most people would not only have heard of it, but may also have taken a dubious "are you left or right brained?" test on social media ... when not looking at funny cat videos.

According to the theory of left-brain or right-brain dominance, each side (or hemisphere) of our brain controls different types of thinking, and people are said to show an innate preference for one thinking style over the other. The left brainers are the logical geeky types, like your engineers or IT guys who get shit done, while the right brainers are your conceptual, creative types, the kind of people who like to draw and riff over pretty diagrams as they work out whether the shit being done is the right shit.

In 2013, Neuroscientists from the University of Utah debunked this model via an extensive two-year study involving 1,011 people between the ages of 7 and 29. Using Functional Magnetic Resonance Imaging (fMRI), they found that both hemispheres of the brain are used equally in all people (Nielsen, Zielinski, Ferguson, Lainhart, & Anderson, 2013).

But this leaves us with a mystery: geeks are still geeks and hippies still hippies. Besides, we have all experienced the pleasures and pains of working with the extreme "left brained" or "right brained" people.

So what is really going on here?

Recent research in the area of neuroscience has started to shed light on this question. A 2014 article, with the riveting title, "Antagonistic neural networks underlying differentiated leadership roles" (Boyatzis, Rochford, & Jack, 2014), describes a link between leadership style and an "antagonistic relationship between two large-scale cortical networks that is present in every individual."

This paper is really interesting, but with a title and tagline like that, we can understand why you might not have heard of it. So being the marketing geniuses we are, we've used the ideas of Chapter 1 to come up with an explanatory model that is guaranteed to bring us in consultancy cash. We call it the "Awati and Culmsee 'Fat Kid on a Seesaw' Model of Problem Solving".

Here is the basic idea: the authors of the paper claimed there is an inherent tension between empathetic thinking vs. analytic reasoning. When the parts of the brain that deal with task oriented work (i.e. work requiring logical thought) are activated, the brain's ability to think empathetically is inhibited … and vice-versa. This means it is hard for people to be empathetic and analytic/task oriented *at the same time*. In short, it's much like how a seesaw works: when one side is up, the other is down.

It seems that all humans have this cognitive seesaw inside their heads.

Boyatzis and his colleagues suggested that this seesaw translates to leadership styles. Leaders tend to be *either* task-oriented or socio-emotionally oriented. It is not so much a question of how to be both at the same time because, like a seesaw, the activated mode tends to dominate the other. A better way to think about it is that ideally, a person should have the ability to *pivot* at will between these two modes of thinking … and more about this in a moment.

So how does this mental seesaw manifest itself in the human brain? The two pathways in the brain that govern this are called the Task-Positive Network (TPN) and the Default Mode Network (DMN). The TPN is activated in task related activities that involve focusing of attention, logical and mathematical reasoning, making decisions, and control of action—in other words, it is handy for getting things done. On the other hand, the DMN plays a central role in emotional self-awareness, thinking about one's own and others' mental states, social cognition and ethical decision making. According to the paper, it is also strongly linked to creativity and insightful problem solving.

It appears that while the idea of left and right hemispheres of the brain controlling proceedings has been debunked, evidence indicates humans have a natural disposition toward either analytical-mechanical reasoning (TPN) or social-relational reasoning (DMN). In other words: *there is a skinny kid at one end of our mental seesaws and a fat kid at the other.* Perhaps the left vs right brain brigade can have the last laugh after all. For although they did not get the underlying cause right (and therefore

t construct is wrong), the observation they are trying to
people have a natural proclivity for one style of thinking
r—is consistent with this new explanation.

& Co came to the fairly obvious conclusion that, when
leaders take a task-oriented approach, their ability and desire to attend to
the relationship needs of their followers is diminished. Therefore, an
over-emphasis on task-oriented leadership can cause problems when
openness to new ideas, people, emotions, and ethical concerns are
important to success. Similarly, an over-emphasis on relationship-
oriented leadership may prove detrimental to keeping people focused on
the execution of clearly defined goals.

Complicating matters further, in the inconveniently messy real
world, leadership always involves both task-based work *and* social/ethical
considerations. For situations where the most productive approach is
unclear or ambiguous, people tend to rely on the mode that is in line with
their dispositions. This leads to the problem of leaders getting "stuck" in
one mode, which suppresses their ability to switch between the two
networks when they most need to do so. Since we have all been that
skinny kid stuck at the top of seesaw while the bigger kid at the bottom
laughs at us and won't let us down, we can well imagine how hard it can
be for people to switch modes when required to do so. The story of
Edwin from Chapter 2 is a case in point.

Of course, this is not just a leadership issue. If all humans are ruled
by a fat kid on their mental seesaws, the question arises as to what we
can do about it. Boyatzis & Co stress the need to train ourselves to
recognise the situation at hand and switch between the task and
relationship (socio-emotional) modes as needed. They suggest that with
enough practice, it should become easier and quicker to pivot between
the two networks with reduced cognitive effort. In other words, the
skinny kid goes to the gym and bulks up while the fat kid does cardio
and goes on a diet, thereby allowing our seesaw to swing more evenly
without visiting extremes.

"Leaders with certain social competencies require less
cognitive effort to complete a social task than those
without these competencies, resulting in less activation

of the DMN and less suppression of the TPN. This reduction in the difference or gap between the two networks should make switching between the two networks faster and less costly" (p. 10).

To get our seesaw kids in better shape, Boyatzis & Co suggest training people to high levels of competence in each by enacting the roles requiring each network and getting them to recognize contexts and cues that might require a switch between modes. In theory, this avoids people remaining "stuck in set" and applying an ineffective cognitive strategy for the task at hand.

This is easy to say of course, and is no different from what the left/right brain crowd have been saying for years. While they might have had the precise neural processes wrong, the implications of this new theory are not that far from famous (and bestselling) supermodels like Debono's "Thinking Hats", Covey's "Seven Habits" and Senge's "Fifth Discipline", all of which encourage broader modes of thinking that, in theory, should get our cognitive seesaws seesawing properly.

But Chapters 1 and 2 showed us that despite the books, training courses, certifications and ever-present models, and despite a century of learning about this thing called management, the reality is when a situation is unclear or stressful, people still have out-of-shape kids on their mental seesaws and all of that good advice goes out the window.

Why? Our radical claim is that this happens because of ambiguity ... as well as teddy bears and fetishes!

Teddy bears? Fetishes?? Bet we have your attention now! So let's see if we can justify our claim, starting with the first point: ambiguity.

Ambiguity starts early

Paul's eleven-year-old son Liam, recently went to his first ever school disco and was confronted with the stress and anxiety of sixth grade social complexity. One of the girls in his class had asked him to be her partner for the evening, but via the school grapevine, he had heard rumours that another girl—one who as he put it, "at least 3 other boys in the class like"—wanted to go with him.

What a dilemma this presented! If Liam declined the offer of the first girl, he would potentially hurt her feelings. He was not certain the second girl really wanted to go with him. If he summoned up his courage and asked the second girl to be his partner, she might say no. On the other hand, if he said yes to the first girl, he might miss out on the opportunity to be the envy of the other boys in the class.

Life can be tough when you are eleven.

This is a classic example of a decision with a healthy dose of ambiguity. Up until now, most of Liam's decisions were based on risk alone, which really are not that stressful. The difference between risk and ambiguity is that with risk, the important variables are known and the probability associated with them can be confidently estimated based on prior history. For example, Liam knows full well when bedtime is, and uses past assessments of his parents' reactions to his delay tactics to determine how much extra time he can get away with. He also has a pretty good idea of the quota of vegetables he needs to eat before his parents will let him leave the table. But his dilemma involving two girls was something new, with no precedent and important information missing.

So what can Liam's dilemma teach us about organisational life? In short, it tells us that making decisions in ambiguity-laden situations seem to be much harder than situations involving uncertainty that can be quantified (i.e. *risk*). This is not new of course, as it has been known for many years that people prefer to bet on events they know more about. This is sometimes called the ambiguity effect bias. A famous and often cited example of the ambiguity effect is Ellsberg's urn problem (1961). Imagine two urns, with the first containing 50 red and 50 black balls and the second containing 100 balls in an unknown combination of red and black. Many people prefer to bet on red or black from urn one (a known probability) rather than betting on red or black from urn two which is unknown.

Imaginary ball filled urns are one thing, real life quite another. If we take the notion of the complex social interactions of the 6th grade classroom and apply it to the sea of humanity known as "work", we find lots more ambiguity. Many decisions have to be made with not only imperfect information, but also involve people with differing ideas on what is important, what the solution should be and how it should be implemented.

Does this make me look fat?

So what does ambiguity do to the brain? Various studies have looked into how the brain handles risk versus ambiguity (Hsu, Bhatt, Adolphs, Tranel, & Camerer, 2005; Hsu, 2004). Like the previous study which inspired our fat kid on the cognitive seesaw model, fMRI was used to image people's brains as they performed various tasks involving different degrees of risk and ambiguity. The logic of the researchers was straightforward...

> "If ambiguity does not matter, then the same brain regions should be activated in risky and ambiguous decision. If ambiguity does matter, then differences in regional activation can provide empirical constraints about which theories are on the right track" (Hsu, 2004, p. 1).

Interestingly, to validate their fMRI findings, they also used behavioural data from patients who had lesions in certain areas of the brain. Now we will get to that in a moment, but let's look at the MRI findings first. Hsu et. al. (2005, p. 1680) tell us that:

> "Using functional brain imaging, we show that the level of ambiguity in choices correlates positively with activation in the amygdala and orbitofrontal cortex, and negatively with a striatal system. Moreover, striatal activity correlates positively with expected reward."

Admittedly, we are not all neuroscientists, so to understand the significance of these findings, it's worth examining briefly what each of these areas of the brain are known to regulate:

- The amygdala is involved in many of our emotions and motivations, particularly those that are related to survival, such as fear, anger, and pleasure.
- The orbitofrontal cortex enables individuals to adapt their behaviour in response to unexpected rewards or adversities.
- The dorsal striatum mediates perceptions of causes, effects and rewards when choosing a course of action (Balleine, Delgado, & Hikosaka, 2007).

In view of the above, it appears that a state of ambiguity enhances emotional responses and suppresses logical ones, which leads to a feeling of anxiety, where people can find themselves caught in a *double-bind* (Bateson, Jackson, Haley, & Weakland, 1956)—a *"damned if you do, damned if you don't"* situation, much like a child feels when urged by a parent to "act spontaneously". Another classic example of ambiguity leading to anxiety, often used by stand-up comedians to get a laugh, is the terror a husband feels when his wife asks "Does this make me look fat?" or "Do you think [insert the name of a mutual female acquaintance] is attractive?" Thus we have the "Culmsee and Awati 'Does This Make Me Look Fat?' Model of Decision Making"—which we will invoke at various times in this book.

Now let's get to the non fMRI tests done with patients with lesions. In the experiments, the patients were split into two control groups. While the two groups had similar aetiology, IQ, mathematical ability, and displayed similar performances on other background tasks, one group had orbitofrontal cortex lesions whereas the other group had temporal lobe damage (note that the temporal lobe did not show activation during the fMRI experiments done by Hsu and Co).

As you might have guessed, the group with orbitofrontal cortex lesions were risk and ambiguity-neutral, treating decisions involving ambiguity as they would any other decisions. In the words of Hsu and Co:

"Neurological subjects with orbitofrontal lesions were insensitive to the level of ambiguity and risk in behavioural choices" (p. 1680).

In other words, these patients would happily answer "Yeah, you do look fat in that dress … and your friend is totally hot too," without batting an eyelid. The comparison group (the one with temporal lobe damage) however, appeared to be risk and ambiguity averse like everybody else.

The simple conclusion from this experiment is that, cognitively speaking, ambiguity has the ability to push emotional buttons in such a way as to make us uncomfortable or anxious. As the work described above suggests, different areas of the brain are activated by ambiguous and unambiguous situations. Moreover, it appears that our reaction to ambiguity is an innate human characteristic, *it is how we are wired*. Indeed, all of us have experienced situations like the eleven year-old dealing with the dilemma of who to take to the disco. It is akin to the feeling of dread when faced with making an important career choice, entering into a difficult conversation, an emotionally charged situation or having to work in a toxic work environment—such feelings are debilitating. Little wonder that people faced with such situations would want to go back to their happy place, their haven of psychological equilibrium and stability.

Tolerating ambiguity...

It has long been recognised that some people have a much harder time with ambiguity than others. Indeed, research in this area started in the 1940s and continues to this day. Katya Stoycheva (2011) characterised ambiguity intolerance as follows:

"People who are intolerant of ambiguity perceive and interpret ambiguous situations as a source of psychological discomfort or a threat and tend to avoid them either psychologically (by ignoring ambiguity) or operationally (by leaving the situation). Those who are tolerant of ambiguity are better able to meet the challenge: they can withstand the discomfort of an ambiguous situation long enough to accommodate and generate more appropriate and flexible responses to it" (p. 66).

Over the years, ambiguity tolerance has been examined in the light of individual behavioural factors, cultural factors (how the environment affects ambiguity tolerance) and more recently, in terms of how cognitive and neurological factors influence it. The latter has led to some controversial conjectures. For example, some researchers have suggested that individuals to the right of the political spectrum (conservatives) are more cognitively rigid and less tolerant of ambiguity than individuals to the left (liberals) (Jost, Kruglanski, Glaser, & Sulloway, 2003). Various forms of cognitive tests have been devised to back up such claims. Furthermore, studies have shown that organisational psychopaths[10] have similar fMRI results in the amygdala to the aforementioned patients with lesions. The findings are intriguing, but the jury is out on how robust they are, so the bottom line is that the factors influencing ambiguity tolerance are not well understood.

That said, there *are* ways to gauge someone's tolerance for ambiguity. Stephen Bochner (1965) identified nine primary behavioural characteristics associated with ambiguity intolerance. Think of your boss (and yourself) as you go through these:

1. Need for categorisation
2. Need for certainty
3. Inability to allow good and bad traits to exist in the same person
4. Acceptance of attitude statements representing a white-black view of life
5. A preference for familiar over unfamiliar
6. Rejection of the unusual or different
7. Resistance to reversal of fluctuating stimuli

---

[10] See https://goo.gl/54Jjud for example.

8. Early selection and maintenance of one solution in an ambiguous situation
9. Premature closure

He also identified secondary ambiguity intolerance characteristics. These include:

1. Authoritarian
2. Dogmatic
3. Rigid
4. Closed minded
5. Uncreative
6. Anxious

In reading the above characteristics, readers may be reminded of colleagues, friends and perhaps themselves. For sure, we have worked with colleagues who we would consider ambiguity intolerant, and many of them tend to display behaviours described above. Especially common are traits like "early selection and maintenance of one solution" and "premature closure". But the stereotypical image of the crusty old traditionalist, the task obsessed project manager, or the nervous middle manager with a bad comb-over is just scratching the surface. Depending on which end of the seesaw one's fat kid is on (the task-oriented or socio-emotional end), characteristics like the *need for categorisation* and *need for certainty* as well as *dogmatism*, *anxiety* and *preference for the familiar* tend to manifest themselves in vastly different ways. This subtle point merits a closer look…

The escape to whiteboard reality

Usually it's the so-called left-brainers who come in for the most criticism about ambiguity intolerance because of their propensity to move to action prematurely or choose and stick to the first idea that comes to their heads. Psychologists label this the "need for cognitive closure" and it has been studied extensively (Webster & Kruglanski, 1994). However, it seems to us that right brainers are just as anxious as their left brained comrades—it's just that they are a bit better at hiding their anxieties. They will no doubt disagree with us, so let's see if we can justify our claim.

Robert Chia and Robin Holt (2008) argued that university business schools privileged knowledge-by-representation—theories, concepts and conceptual models—over practical knowledge (they called it knowledge by exemplification, but you could also consider this as lived experience or tacit knowledge). They claimed this imbalance privileged *"detached contemplation over involved action."* Indeed, most models and supermodels that come of management research—which we critiqued in Chapter 1— are outcomes of such detached contemplation, which invariably excludes real-life complexities. Chia and Holt echoed precisely this point...

> "...the fluctuations, modifications, and accidents of actual managerial situations that may enrich any knowledge claim are inevitably excluded, since the representational models adopted are ill-equipped to deal with the intentions and inclinations of people with particular historically and culturally shaped predispositions, intellectual orientations, common sense behaviors, and moral traditions. The particularities of history and circumstance imply the possibility of idiosyncrasy; common sense implies the possibility of tacit, unspoken, inarticulate, and often unmeasurable understanding; and tradition implies the possibility of cultural mediation and contextual distinctiveness, all of which do not lend themselves readily to a universal causal explanation" (p. 475).

Some systems thinkers (and particularly, complex systems theorists) can be the worst offenders in that they indulge in excessive diagram-drawing and hyperbole. Fred Collopy, a student of systems thinking pioneer Russell Ackoff, and teacher of Systems Thinking, wrote an article in 2009 as a warning to Design Thinking[11] aficionados. In the article, entitled "Lessons Learned — Why the Failure of Systems Thinking Should Inform the Future of Design Thinking" (Collopy, 2009), he spoke of attending a two day Systems Thinking workshop at Wharton in which most of the time was spent explaining the heavy conceptual baggage going under the label of "foundational knowledge". In his words:

> "It is a reflection of what has become of systems thinking that it took most of the two days for the facilitator to explicate all that he thought we needed to know before we could begin either critiquing or applying the ideas. In addition to obvious material on the nature of systems, we learned about chaos theory, living systems theory, Santiago theories, [we have cut out a heap more concepts … seriously], the laws of complexity, loops and feedback and more."

Two days of concepts? Could it be that staying in the safe "whiteboard reality" world of concepts, models and frameworks, as opposed to "real reality" is just as much an anxiety coping mechanism for right brainers as all those excruciatingly prescribed and documented processes are for those much-maligned left brainers? Remember Katya Stoycheva's statement that people tend to avoid ambiguous situations either psychologically by ignoring it or operationally by leaving the situation? We feel that for some people talking feels good, feels safe and is a way to leave the situation—as paradoxical as that sounds. Both of us have worked with highly conceptual people who have an amazing ability to avoid taking action while sounding like they are actually doing something.

For such cognitive types, anxiety kicks in when they have to move to action. Way back in 1955, AR Cohen and his colleagues labelled this as the "need for cognition" and argued that someone with a strong need for cognition views "a situation as ambiguous even if it is relatively

---

[11] http://www.fastcompany.com/919258/design-thinking-what

structured, indicating that higher standards for cognitive clarity are associated with greater need for cognition" (Cohen, Stotland, & Wolfe, 1955, p. 292). In other words, the need for cognition is an ambiguity coping mechanism[12].

Speaking of moving to action, and taking due consideration of Cohen and his colleagues, here is another juicy quote from Collopy's (2009) article on how to avoid the mistakes of the systems thinking movement.

> "What is the alternative? I would suggest that we should focus instead on building and describing an arsenal of methods and techniques, many of them drawn from various extant design practices that are applicable to the domains and problems in questions. Describing these techniques as well as the conditions under which each is of value would constitute an invaluable program of research."

The notion of "conditions" is very interesting and we will examine it in great detail in the following chapters. We also think Collopy is absolutely right when he talks about "an arsenal of techniques." There is no "one best method or practice to rule them all", so not only do practitioners need to know a variety of them, they also need the smarts to figure out which ones are appropriate to the situation at hand. We will give you some practical tips on this in Chapter 7. For now, we simply note that Chia and Holt made a similar plea to Collopy by suggesting that people need to face ambiguity head on, embrace it and darn well learn to cope with it:

> "…mastery of the art of management can only be accomplished if 'the detached information-consuming stance of the novice … is replaced by (an emotional) involvement' in which the student experiences a deep

---

[12] Since then, the term has been modified in literature to represent someone who is ambiguity tolerant—probably through detached contemplation!

sense of personal vulnerability. In other words, direct subjective experiencing of the consequences of one's actions and decisions, both errors and achievements, are vital to the mastery of a practical skill such as management" (Chia & Holt, 2008, p. 478).

In other words, stop being a wuss, get in, get your hands dirty and live with the consequences! Sounds like good advice for getting our cognitive seesaw kids in better shape as well as for dealing with "does this make me look fat?" situations.

Now we fully expect some readers at this point to feel a tad indignant. There are plenty of examples where people use a model, concept or a prescriptive process to help clarify an ambiguous situation and end up delivering great outcomes while facilitating deep learning. We do not disagree with this at all. What we are suggesting is that *if reducing anxiety is the primary driver, it can preclude the sort of learning that is really needed.* Instead a sort of *anti-learning* occurs, a systematic learning of the wrong lessons. To make matters more complex, *many people who are driven by anxiety reduction are wholly unaware of this anti-learning.*

So what happens if anxiety driven anti-learning is allowed to fester? As you might imagine, it's not good…

From anxiety to social defences

In the late 1950s, Isabel Menzies Lyth spent time in a London teaching hospital, helping to diagnose the causes of problems they were having with trainee nurses. The work environment was toxic and a third of student nurses left before completing their training, usually at their own request. Amongst those who stayed and qualified, turnover was high, morale low and absenteeism higher than the industry norm.

Menzies Lyth found the root cause was that the anxiety created by the harsh reality of close involvement with patients, drove defensive behaviours in nurses. Interestingly, she also found that these defence mechanisms were for the most part *ineffective*. Nevertheless, they had become embedded in the cultural and operational fabric of the organisation. She called these mechanisms *social defences* (Menzies Lyth, 1960) and the ones she observed included:

- **Breaking up the work of care into tasks across multiple patients:** In other words, nurses did a specific task for multiple patients rather providing in-depth care to a single patient. No one nurse was completely responsible for one patient.

- **Depersonalising and detachment:** A culture of nurses discussing patients by bed number or illness, rather than their names. Mary Jones became "the liver in room ten."

- **Reducing decision making by a ritualistic approach to tasks:** Processes and tasks were precisely detailed and student nurses were actively discouraged from taking their own initiative. One example cited was about a nurse who had been told to give a patient with a sleeping disorder, sleeping medication at a certain time. One day, when his medication was due, the patient had already fallen into a deep, natural sleep. However, obeying orders the nurse woke him up and gave him the medicine, despite her common sense and judgement telling her to leave him alone.

- **Reducing weight and responsibility of decision making by excessive checks and counter-checks:** Excessive consultation was done prior to any decision making, even for trivial situations.

- **Purposeful obscurity in definition of roles and responsibilities:** Quoting from Menzies "Responsibility and authority on wards were generalised in a way that made them non-specific and prevented them falling firmly on one person … This was a policy for inactivity"

- **Delegating in reverse:** Tasks frequently were forced upwards so that all responsibility for performance could be avoided.

- **Avoidance of change:** Change was actively resisted and tended to be made only in times of crisis.

Given the continued high levels of stress for staff and the high turnover rates, Menzies argued the defences that had embedded themselves into process and culture were self-defeating *because the underlying anxiety remained.* In fact, the problem was aggravated because nurses who remained in the hospital came to view these mechanisms as part of their professional identity, which further legitimised these practices. No prizes for guessing what happened when the next generation of nurses were trained.

Given that Menzies Lyth was reporting serious systemic issues with the practice of nursing at that time, it might not surprise you that management of the hospital pretty much rejected her findings. We can only assume it made them feel anxious! Bain (1998) reported that the Nursing Times magazine called it a "devastating criticism of the nursing service" and attempted to refute it.

The reaction to the study highlights how hard it can be to disrupt social defences once they are established. Worse, the illusion of certainty and safety provided by such mechanisms preclude genuine organisational learning. "That's not how we do things around here" is a very common refrain in such organisations, as is having to deal with the "thought police", "corporate immune mechanism" or the "unmentionable" elephants in the room—various "organisational defence routines" (Argyris, 1990) that are so common in organisation-land. Reflecting on Menzies Lyth's work in 2010, James Krantz (2010) astutely noted:

> "What makes social defences so effective is that either they eliminate situations that expose people to anxiety-provoking activity altogether or they insulate people from the consequences of their actions" (p. 193).

On teddy bears and fetishes

Since the pioneering work of Isabel Menzies Lyth, many others have written about the power of social defences in different organisational settings. The best known would be Chris Argyris, who became very well known for his work on defensive reasoning and organisational defence routines. Among the lesser-known work in this area is a paper by David Wastell (1996) entitled "The Fetish of Technique: Methodology as a Social Defence". This paper can be uncomfortable reading for IT types. Not only did Wastell argue compellingly that methodologies (such as those used in project management or software development) have the propensity to function as social defences against anxiety, he went a step further and labelled them as *fetishes*—and who can resist that, eh?

Wastell expanded on social defences by connecting them to the notion of a *transitional object*. This concept was first described by the famed paediatrician, Donald Winnicott (1953), who described how such objects are crucial to the development of independence and self-reliance in children. Examples of transitional objects include security blankets and teddy bears. In general terms, a transitional object can be anything that facilitates intellectual and emotional development by providing a temporary source of support which enables the learner to "let go" of a former, dependent relationship. As an example, Paul's daughter Ashlee had a teddy bear named "Toby", who had to accompany her on many sleepovers when she was young. If Toby was accidentally left behind, there was absolutely no way Ashlee was going to sleep in an unfamiliar place. As she grew older and more independent, she no longer needed Toby to accompany her.

Wastell noted that a broad range of entities can function as transition objects for adults. These could be inanimate (e.g. a model, methodology, idea, theory, or indeed a work-practice) or human (a teacher, management guru, or consultant). He specifically targeted methodologies and suggested that novices initially used them because they provided psychological support, much in the same way as a child depends on a transitional object like a teddy bear.

This in itself is not an issue, as Wastell stated:

> "...the novice is emboldened to tackle and to solve the problems in the world. As experience grows, self-confidence grows and the technique is used with increasing discretion and flexibility. Ultimately the methodology is internalised and becomes invisible; The novice has become the expert. The transitional object

has served its purpose and like a crutch is discarded" (p. 34).

The imagery of a crutch is apt, given that the point is to eventually discard it and start walking on one's own. But here is the rub: if the process of development is *disrupted* in some way—for example, an organisational environment where anxiety driven defensive mechanisms run rampant—an unhealthy dependence on the transitional object can develop. That is, the crutch becomes a fetish that cannot be let go.

Now, a lot of people will hear the word fetish and think of the sexual connotations of the term, however what it means here is an object or procedure used with a pathological intensity for *its own sake, not as a means to an end.* It is in this sense that Wastell argued that methodology can become a fetish object. The rigid, mechanistic implementation of a methodology provides a relief against anxiety by "insulating the practitioner from the risks and uncertainties of real engagement with people and problems" (p. 34).

In other words, methodology becomes an organisational defence mechanism.

Conclusion

Wastell claimed that transitional objects can take a variety of forms. When you think about it, many of the titles in the non-fiction section of a typical bookstore are in a sense, anxiety alleviators. Consider the content of self-help books, or those on leadership, motivation, change management, project management, process improvement, decision making, organisational development, complexity theory, Lean, Six Sigma, and systems thinking, to name just a small selection. While they are about very different things, all present models and methods that help us cope with situations involving a healthy dose of ambiguity.

However, as we have learnt in this chapter, not only will the fat kid on the seesaw influence one's choice of book, but if anxiety reduction is the primary driver, chances are good that the techniques described in the book of choice will be used in a fetishised way. That is, they will be used as anxiety-reduction mechanisms, and will do so at the expense of true learning and development. In short, whether you are left brained engineer or a right brained hippie, any model you choose has the potential to morph into a defensive mechanism, thereby undermining its original intent. It is only fair we warn you this is true of this book as well!

To put it all in terms of our simple model, perhaps practitioners need to ask themselves whether they truly have the courage to offer an honest answer to a "Do I look fat in this?" kind of question.

4

What a Bunch of Needy Types

[*plotting ways to kill Kuzco*]
Yzma: Ah, how shall I do it? Oh, I know. I'll turn him into a flea, a harmless, little flea, and then I'll put that flea in a box, and then I'll put that box inside of another box, and then I'll mail that box to myself, and when it arrives…
[*laughs*]
Yzma: …I'll smash it with a hammer! It's brilliant, brilliant, brilliant, I tell you! Genius, I say!
[*knocks over bottle of poison on flower, which shrivels up and dies*]
Yzma: Or, to save on postage, I'll just poison him with this.

—Emperor's New Groove

How does James Bond survive?

How is it that James Bond has stayed alive long enough to star in so many movies? After all, he is continually facing adversaries who are rich, evil geniuses with prodigious intellects and virtually unlimited resources at their disposal. Yet Bond manages to survive the odds, save the day, kill the evil genius ... and to add insult to injury, steal the criminal mastermind's supermodel girlfriend too.

The endless box office potential of Bond movies arises from a fatal flaw in the psyche of the evil geniuses depicted in them. The clearest articulation of the flaw is provided by Mike Meyers in one of his Austin Powers movies. In case you haven't seen the series, the bad guy is "Dr Evil". Here's the relevant exchange between the good doctor and his son, Scott.

- **Dr. Evil:** Scott, I want you to meet Daddy's nemesis, Austin Powers.
- **Scott:** Why don't you just kill him?
- **Dr. Evil:** No, Scott, I have a better idea. I'm going to place him in an easily escapable situation involving an overly elaborate and exotic death.
- **Scott:** Why don't you shoot him now? I mean, come on, I'll go get a gun. We'll shoot him together. It'll be fun. BANG! Dead. Done.
- **Dr. Evil:** One more peep out of you and you are grounded, mister! And I am not joking!

Had evil geniuses heeded the advice of folks like Scott, James Bond would not have made it past Dr. No[13] ... and the world at large would not have enjoyed (or suffered) an endless parade of Bond movies.

One has to conclude that for all their smarts, evil mega-geniuses are actually pretty dumb.

---

[13] The first Bond Movie.

This begs the question as to what makes someone intelligent. If Dr Evil took an IQ test, he would probably be off the chart. Similarly, if you have watched the popular sitcom Big Bang Theory, you will be familiar with Dr Sheldon Cooper, the brilliant theoretical physicist with a towering intellect. Sheldon's IQ is so high that it "cannot be accurately measured by normal tests" (as he so eloquently puts it). He is more than happy to remind all and sundry just how brilliant he is. In truth, the only thing bigger than his IQ is his level of social ineptitude.

It is likely that most of our readers would have met organisational smarty-pants like Sheldon Cooper, and perhaps a few Dr Evil types as well. More to the point, it is very likely that you've been on the receiving end of dumb decisions from smart people. As we wrote these words, we googled "university professor scandal" and found a variety of transgressions from academic fraud to sleaze (for what it's worth, the 3rd result was entitled "HIV Cure Scandal: Rabbit-Based Cure Research Faked" and as for sleaze, the less said the better).

Now we are not here to pick on university professors. We chose them because we figured a population of academics would have a significant number of people with high IQs. We could have picked pretty much any other profession and added the word "scandal" to it, to find a sea of poor judgement, irrational thinking and salacious reading to boot.

Imagine then, if we could measure *quality of judgement* in the same way that IQ can be measured. Such a test would essentially be an assessment of a person's decision-making ability. We could call it the "You might be smart but you're still an idiot" test or perhaps as a tribute to flawed evil geniuses we could call it the "Can you kill James Bond?" test.

It turns out that such a test might just be possible. But before we get to that, let's take a whirlwind tour of some of the psychological factors that impact our decision making abilities.

In the introductory chapter of our last book, we quoted a piece called "The Plan" which highlights how a message gets distorted as it moves up the organisational hierarchy. Here it is in full...

"In the beginning was the plan
And then came the assumptions
And the assumptions were without form

And the plan was completely without substance
And darkness was upon the faces of the workers
And they spake unto their marketing managers, saying `it is a pot of
manure, and it stinketh'
And the marketing managers went unto the strategists and saith,
`It is a pile of dung, and none may abide the odor thereof'.
And the strategists went unto the business managers and saith
`It is a container of excrement, and it is very strong and such that
none may abide by it'.
And the business managers went unto the director and saith,
`It is a vessel of fertilizer, and none may abide its strength'.
And the director went to the vice president and saith,
`It contains that which aids plant growth and it is very strong'.
And the vice president went unto the senior vice president and saith,
`It promoteth growth, and it is powerful'.
And the senior vice president went unto the president and saith,
`This powerful new plan will actively promote growth and efficiency
of the company and the business in general'.
And the president looked upon the plan and saw that it was good
And the plan became policy"

We also mentioned Thomas Keating (2009), who asserted that
humans have three instinctual needs: *safety and security*; *approval and esteem*
and; *power and control*. You can see these needs in action in "The Plan"
where the message conveyed is subtly altered as it moves up the
organisational hierarchy. For example, someone with safety and security
needs might subconsciously or consciously ask themselves "If I say this,
will I lose my job?" and as a consequence, change the message in a way
that suits them. Similarly, folks with approval and esteem needs might
ask "If I say this, what will people think of me?" and those with power
and control needs might ask "If I say this, what might I gain or lose?"

Keating conceptualised safety, approval/esteem and power/control
as *instinctual* needs—things we are born with. In his view, all three needs
are essentially good, but when unfulfilled or disrupted, can trigger the
development of compensatory mechanisms. Using Keating's model in
the context of James Bond's extreme durability, we might hypothesise

that Dr Evil's innate need for approval and esteem is his blind spot. After all, not only do evil geniuses use much-too-elaborate Rube Goldberg-ish[14] means to kill Bond, they also have a penchant for revealing their evil plans to our hero just before leaving him to his own devices.

What a needy bunch...

Since psychological needs provide a means to understand human behaviour, many psychologists and cognitive researchers have been besotted with identifying and understanding them for close to a century.

Probably the best known is Maslow's hierarchy of needs[15], a bona fide supermodel from the 1940s that has graced many PowerPoint presentations. Maslow (1943) identified *physical health, security, self-esteem, belongingness,* and *self-actualisation* as a *hierarchy of needs.* While Maslow's model is popular, there are many other notable theories that never achieved supermodel status. McClelland (1953) for example, claimed that the most important motivators are *achievement, authority/power* and *affiliation.* Self Determination Theory speaks of *autonomy, relatedness* and *competence* (Deci & Ryan, 2008). Although it lacks a nice visualisation to compete with Maslow, it is popular in some circles because it has strong empirical backing. Belongingness theory boils it down to ... well ... the need to belong (Baumeister & Leary, 1995). Sirota, Mischkind, & Meltzer (2005) came up with a model that has a distinctly organisational flavour. They identified *equity/fairness, achievement* and *camaraderie* as the key factors (we could keep going all day but we trust you get the idea).

With such a smorgasbord of needs and models to choose from, one can only conclude that either humans are really, really *needy* or that a lot of these needs overlap. To that end, Sheldon (*not* Sheldon Cooper) and his colleagues described what at first glance seems like a reality TV show. In a paper we colloquially labelled "'Psychological Needs Survivor", he

---

[14] https://en.wikipedia.org/wiki/Rube_Goldberg_machine
[15] Aspiring management gurus should take note that Maslow's needs model was initially a run-of-the-mill management model when he first came up with it (Maslow, 1943). It did not achieve supermodel status until he used the "Pyramid

and his colleagues mined the various theories for the top 10 "candidate psychological needs" and then devised experiments to see which ones were "voted off the island" so to speak (Sheldon, 2001). Their findings were consistent with the needs predicted by Self-Determination Theory (*autonomy*, *relatedness* and *competence*), but also added *self-esteem* to the mix.

Self-defeated by the smart dumb guy

Rather than get caught up in a long-winded game of "compare and contrast psychological needs", we would rather draw your attention to a common theme that runs through them. When these needs are thwarted, individuals resort to coping strategies that can be *self-defeating*. While we have already learnt about the self-defeating behaviours of criminal mega-geniuses trying to kill James Bond in reel-life, there are many more examples from real-life. Here are some common ones that often show up in the workplace:

- The tormented genius who is frustrated that people cannot see his awesomeness, despite his constant attempts to show people how smart he is.
- The serial micromanager who finds that subordinates are unwilling to make decisions, and therefore ends up micromanaging them even more.
- The person who always has to be right, and when she is not, moves the semantic goal posts so that the argument is no longer the original argument and therefore she technically isn't wrong.
- The perennial victim who believes that the entire organisation conspires to prevent him from advancing, but when given opportunities to advance, finds excuses to avoid taking them … thereby making him feel evermore victimised.

Noir" look in a book released a decade later (Maslow 1954). This famous pyramid diagram made it particularly easy to grasp, explain, and toss into a PowerPoint presentation

Sometimes people who exhibit such behaviours are not the most popular kids in the organisational playground. In extreme cases they may find themselves being avoided or excluded because others find these behaviours annoying or denying them *their* psychological needs. For example, the micromanager's behaviour subverts employees' needs for autonomy and sense of being in control, so employees respond by withdrawing their discretionary effort and adopting transactional behaviours that sidestep the need to make decisions. This creates a vicious circle because the underlying anxiety that drives these self-defeating behaviours is not addressed. At an organisational level, such behaviours can manifest themselves as dysfunctions such as the one illustrated in "The Plan". No single individual can be blamed for the gap between the coal-face and the executive suite, but all contribute to it in their own way.

The net result of this is similar to the self-defeating practices of the nurses from the 1958 study we examined in the last chapter. If you recall, we saw *institutionalised* poor practices such as avoidance of change, applying ritualistic approaches to tasks, excess application of checks and balances, purposeful lack of role clarity and excess delegation of decision-making. As anyone who has worked in a mid to large-sized organisation will attest to, such practices are alive and well even today.

Psychological needs are not the whole story; there is yet another spanner in our thought-works. In terms of the example we started with, James Bond might survive an encounter with a criminal genius for reasons that have nothing to do with psychological needs. Even if a criminal genius' psychological needs are satisfied and he becomes a well-adjusted criminal *mega*-genius who is savvy enough to avoid using overly elaborate mechanisms to kill James Bond, our hero might yet live.

Why? Because of *cognitive biases.*

Barriers to good judgement

While "spot the psychological need" is a popular research area, "find another cognitive bias" is even more of an academic sport. In our earlier book, we devoted an entire chapter to the topic of cognitive bias, focusing on the pioneering work of Nobel Prize winner, Daniel Kahneman. In the time between that book and this one, Kahneman published his best-seller "Thinking Fast and Slow" (2011) and introduced the world to the myriad ways that human judgement is susceptible to various kinds of bias. As a result, awareness of bias has increased. Wikipedia, for example, has a huge list of biases[16] and we have listed some here so you get the idea:

- **Ambiguity Effect:** The tendency to select options where the probability of a favourable outcome is known, over an option where the probability of a favourable outcome is unknown. Our urn example in the last chapter is the ambiguity effect in action.

- **Anchoring:** The tendency to rely too heavily on the first piece of information offered (the anchor) when making decisions. This is the bias that keeps pawn shops in business. When negotiating with a seller, a pawnbroker will make an extremely low offer to set the anchor. The bargaining then tends to remain close to the anchor point, with the seller often settling on a price which is lower than what the pawnbroker would have been willing to pay.

- **Confirmation bias:** The tendency of people to favour (or selectively seek) information that confirms their opinions. Another manifestation of this bias is when people interpret information in a way that supports their opinions. This one drives a lot of political debate. Politicians take advantage of this bias on this by selectively presenting data and information that they know will confirm the hopes (or fears) of their constituents.

- **Loss Aversion:** The tendency to give preference to avoiding losses (even small losses) over making gains. A particularly common manifestation of loss aversion in project environments is the sunk cost bias. For example, throwing good money at a project that is clearly a lost cause.

---

[16] https://en.wikipedia.org/wiki/List_of_cognitive_biases

- **Information bias**: The tendency for people to seek as much data as they can lay their hands on before making a decision, as a result being swamped by too much irrelevant information.
- **The curse of knowledge:** This refers to the difficulty that knowledgeable people have in thinking of problems from the perspective of those who are less well informed.
- **Hipster bias:** The tendency for self-declared non-mainstream middle class bohemians to grow well manicured beards (Okay we snuck that one in ourselves. See our previous book for more fun cognitive biases like this one).

Everyone is subject to these biases, even well-adjusted evil geniuses depicted in 007 movies. For example, hipster bad guys might be vulnerable to using overly elaborate, and hence, easy-to-escape ways to kill Bond because shooting him would be just too mainstream.

Interestingly, much like Bond and his assorted nemeses, the story of cognitive biases has two contrasting elements. Indeed, Kahneman named his book "Thinking Fast and Slow" because it is based on a *dual process theory of cognition.* This theory contends that human cognition works through two distinct mental processes: one which is fast and effortless (called System 1) and the other slow and deliberate (called System 2). Although these two processes work in tandem, they often conflict with each other. We'll explore these next to lay the ground for what comes in the following chapters.

A brief introduction to System 1 and 2

According to Kahneman (2002), System 1 is the brain's fast, automatic, intuitive, and emotional approach and is the first line of cognitive processing. Among other things, it allows you to read these words effortlessly, recognise faces, and multiply 7 by 6 (assuming you were taught your multiplication tables in school). On the other hand, understanding *why* we specifically chose 7 multiplied by 6[17], or answering 187.225 multiplied by 53.7 will likely take you longer and require *focus*. This is because it invokes System 2: the mind's slower, analytical mode in which reason dominates. System 2 is responsible for "executive control", taking System 1's judgments as input. Essentially, System 1 comes with emotional baggage and System 2 tries to compensate for it. In his Nobel Prize lecture, Kahneman said this of System 1 and 2 (emphasis ours):

> "The operations of System 1 are fast, automatic, effortless, associative, *and often emotionally charged; they are also governed by habit, and are therefore difficult to control or modify.* The operations of System 2 are slower, serial, effortful, and deliberately controlled; they are also relatively flexible and potentially rule-governed" (Kahneman D. , 2002).

Cognitive effort is tiring. Anyone who has taken an exam, participated in an all-day strategy workshop or been the skinny kid on the wrong end of a cognitive seesaw will be able to vouch for this. As a result, we tend to accept System 1's advice, overriding it only when we absolutely have to. This explains why all hipsters look the same, and why many (most?) people have a "hot button" that, when pushed, can trigger unexpectedly vehement reactions.

Now it needs to be said that although the phenomenon of cognitive bias has been established empirically, the dual mode theory underlying it is somewhat controversial. Kahneman more-or-less acknowledged this in the conclusion to his book. Consider the following lines:

> "This book has described the workings of the mind as an uneasy interaction between two fictitious characters: the automatic System 1 and the effortful System 2. You are now quite familiar with the personalities of the two systems and able to anticipate how they might respond in

---

[17] No, we are not going to tell you why. Ask someone else ... eventually you will see why!

different situations. And of course you also remember that the two systems do not really exist in the brain or anywhere else. 'System 1 does X' is a shortcut for 'X occurs automatically.' And 'System 2 is mobilized to do Y' is a shortcut for 'arousal increases, pupils dilate, attention is focused, and activity Y is performed.' I hope you find the language of systems as helpful as I do, and that you have acquired an intuitive sense of how they work without getting confused by the question of whether they exist" (Kahneman D. , 2011, p. 415).

Apart from urging readers not to get too caught up in the language he used, Kahneman also stated that he borrowed the terms System 1 and System 2 from early writings of Keith Stanovich and Richard West who he noted "greatly influenced my thinking". Interestingly, Stanovich and West did not find the concept as helpful as Kahneman, and have since moved on. Abandoning the use of "System" to describe cognitive modes, they now suggest a tri-mode process instead of a dual one.

To explain why their thinking evolved along these lines, we first need to better understand what it means to think rationally and make rational judgements.

Intelligence vs rationality (and tin foil hats)

We deliberately started this chapter with an exploration of the minds of criminal mega-geniuses because it highlights how one can be super smart and deeply dumb at the same time. Stanovich and West (2014) sought to resolve the "smart people doing dumb things" paradox by distinguishing between *intelligence* and *rational judgement*. They recommended restricting the notion of intelligence to what IQ tests measure, which is computational/logical prowess and acquired knowledge. This means common concepts like emotional intelligence and social intelligence should be *excluded* from the notion of intelligence. In their view, many of the factors that undermine good judgement are not correlated with increased IQ and therefore *should not* be conflated with it. The problem with using the same term to describe both is nicely summarised by them as follows:

> "In a sense, broad theorists seek to break a rule of construct validity—and of common sense: things that are named the same should go together. If these things really are separate mental faculties, and we wish to emphasize their separateness, then we should not suggest just the opposite by calling them all 'intelligences' " (p. 10).

There are two elements to rational judgement: how well a person's beliefs map to the real world (called *epistemic rationality*)[18] and whether appropriate action is taken given one's goals and beliefs (called *instrumental rationality*)[19].

Epistemic rationality relates to how we form and update our world views. It is the lens through which we form our beliefs regarding what is *true*. As an example, put a creationist and a Darwinist in the room and ask which one of them is telling the truth. Both will be absolutely sincere that their truth is the right one and the other's is wrong. Even science, with its claim to objectivity, warns us that scientific truths are contingent and forever subject to revision in the light of new knowledge. Moreover, some "established" truths can turn out to be based on flawed evidence— the social sciences are particularly prone to this problem, as we will illustrate in the next chapter.

Another way to help understand epistemic rationality is to consider examples of epistemic *irrationality*, such as believing that Elvis is still alive, the Moon landings were a hoax, or that aliens are remote-controlling our thoughts with ESP. The latter example also illustrates the difference between epistemic rationality and its cousin, *instrumental rationality*. If

---

[18] Episteme is a word that comes up a lot in academic literature. For the uninitiated, it can be described as one's knowledge based on one's learning, belief systems, philosophies and tacit assumptions.

[19] We would be remiss to point out that there are other views of rationality. For example, we devoted a chapter to the notion of *communicative rationality* in our previous book (Culmsee & Awati, 2013).

someone really believes they are in danger of being remote controlled by "little green folk" with a penchant for probes, the instrumentally rational thing to do would be to wear a home-made tin-foil hat that would protect the brain from extra-terrestrial cognitive interference. Thus, while this person might be epistemologically irrational, wearing a tin-foil hat is actually instrumentally rational. Instrumental rationality is about taking actions commensurate with your beliefs. More colloquially, it is whether someone "walks their talk".

Stanovich and West suggested that we ought to measure our quality of rational thinking (RQ) independently of measuring intelligence. Such a test should cover both epistemic and instrumental thinking, and be separate from an IQ test. A person could have an IQ of 130 and a RQ of 60. Another might have an IQ of 115 and an RQ of 125. Who would you rather have as your financial planner?

Introducing the reflective brain...

Now that we have examined Stanovich and West's ideas about rationality as a construct distinct from intelligence, we will discuss why they think it makes sense to move from a dual model of cognition (System 1 and System 2) to a tri-state model. First up, rather than using the language of Systems preferred by Kahneman, they based their model around the notions of the *Autonomous Mind*, the *Algorithmic Mind* and the *Reflective Mind* as shown in Figure 4.1.

The autonomous brain is largely unchanged from Kahneman's System 1, which responds automatically to triggering stimuli. System 2 is divided into two parts, based on the distinction between intelligence and rationality we discussed in the last section.

The algorithmic brain (System 2a) is responsible for intelligence as measured by IQ style intelligence tests which focus on *fluid* and *crystallised* intelligence. The former is the ability for abstract reasoning and the ability to recognise patterns (think of those pattern sequences in IQ tests where you have to pick the next one in the sequence). The latter is the ability to make use of acquired information or knowledge, and is measured by vocabulary tasks and verbal comprehension. Dr Evil typically aces both of these kinds of tests.

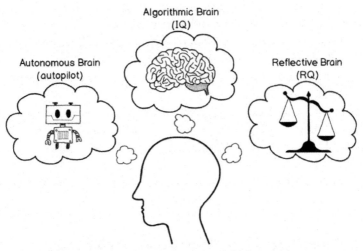

Figure 4.1: The elements of the tri-state model of cognition

The reflective mind (System 2b) is where rationality and belief systems come into play. Stanovich (2009) noted that *ambiguity is resolved differently by individuals with different thinking styles and belief systems*, a point with consequences we will explore at length in Chapter 7. The reflective mind is where judgements are rationally assessed and drive the wearing of tin-foil hats. It is this ability that would be measured by the yet-to-be devised RQ tests. This would leave the IQ tests to focus on what they currently do: measure cognitive abilities related to algorithmic reasoning.

The notion of the reflective brain is an important one. Among other things, it incorporates all the cognitive elements we have examined in Chapters 3 and 4, including ambiguity tolerance, seesaw kids, object fetishes, and defensive routines. In short, the reflective mind reflects one's *thinking disposition*—a term widely used in cognitive psychology to cover a wide range of cognitive behaviours. In the last chapter, we highlighted the difference between the need for cognitive closure (reliance on quick judgement) and the need for cognition (the tendency to think a lot). Both are commonly cited examples of thinking dispositions, but they are far from the only ones. Others include:

- **"Stop, my brain hurts"** disposition, where people find it difficult to cope with multifaceted problems that have no straightforward or clear cut solutions.

- **"I just know"** disposition, characterised by undue confidence in one's own views.

- **"Yes, but what about the children?"** disposition characterised by the tendency to think about future consequences before taking action.

- **"Just give me the facts"** disposition where there is a tendency to calibrate the strength of one's belief based on the quantum of evidence available.

- **"What option scores the highest?"** disposition where there is a tendency to explicitly weigh pros and cons of situations before making a decision.

- **"What are we missing?"** disposition where there is a tendency to seek different viewpoints and avoid absolutism.

It should be clear that the dispositions listed above can serve as advantages or disadvantages depending on the situation at hand. More interestingly, Stanovich (2009) identified various thinking dispositions that *predict the quality (or lack thereof) of rational thinking* (RQ). In Figure 4.2, we list examples of thinking dispositions known to negatively affect judgement. Just for fun, we also list some of Bochner's ambiguity intolerance characteristics examined in Chapter 3 for comparison because we couldn't help but notice the connections between the two.

The fact that thinking dispositions map so closely to characteristics of ambiguity intolerance (or tolerance) suggests that the key to managing ambiguous situations lies in understanding the thinking dispositions of one's audience and framing the ambiguous situation accordingly. We'll say much more about this in Chapter 7, but for now, let's see what else Stanovich and West have to say about the distinction between rationality and intelligence.

Thinking Dispositions (Stanovich and West)	Ambiguity Intolerance Characteristics (Bochner)
Superstition	Anxious, need for certainty[20]
Dogmatism	Dogmatic
Loyalty to beliefs versus loyalty to reality	Acceptance of attitude statements representing a white-black view of life, Closed minded, Rejection of the unusual or different, A preference for familiar over unfamiliar
Overconfidence	Early selection and maintenance of one solution in an ambiguous situation
Insensitivity to contradictions	Inability to allow good and bad traits to exist in the same person, Resistance to reversal of fluctuating stimuli
Need for closure	Premature closure, Need for certainty
Thinking about future consequences	Early selection and maintenance of one solution in an ambiguous situation
Hierarchy of goals	Need for categorisation
Reflective versus impulsive personality	Uncreative

Figure 4.2: Thinking dispositions contrasted with ambiguity intolerance characteristics

Taking a cue from the term "dyslexia", a disorder affecting reading ability despite adequate intelligence, Stanovich (1994, p. 11) coined the term *Dysrationalia* to describe the inability to think and behave rationally, despite adequate intelligence. At the start of this chapter, we mentioned the possibility of measuring a person's quality of judgement and labelled it the "Can you kill James Bond?" test. Indeed, Stanovich's research lab is attempting to create precisely such a test: the "first assessment instrument that will comprehensively measure individual differences in

---

[20] Some superstitions serve as soothers for anxious people and superstitious routines often relate to a false sense of security regarding cause and effect (as in, "If I have my lucky charm, then things will go as I wish them to.")

rational thought" (Stanovich & West, 2014, p. 267). In a nutshell, a test for Dysrationalia.

Are you Dysrational?

Let's pretend Stanovich and West read this book and applied our patented advice for successful model-making. As a result, the Dysrationalia test has achieved supermodel status and is right up there with IQ tests and the Myers Briggs test for personality type. We are willing to bet many readers would feel a tad anxious if such a scenario were to come to pass. Imagine a workplace where staff must take a test to measure their rationality. Would a senior executive team or a board be willing to share their RQ in company annual reports knowing that investors can take it into account when judging the worth of the company?

Would such an instrument mean that smart people who are convinced NASA faked the moon landings, September 11 was an inside job, vaccinations cause autism, Paleo diets are the right path for nutrition, or that the world is secretly being run by a secretive cabal called the Illuminati, consistently display lower RQ scores? More interestingly for us (and perhaps for Stanovich and his colleagues), would ambiguity intolerant people score lower than their ambiguity tolerant counterparts? On the other hand, given what we know via our neuroscience informed "does this make me look fat?" model, would a cold-blooded organisational psychopath do brilliantly?

Some insight into the questions above can be gleaned from what Stanovich sees as the three main causes of Dysrationalia (Stanovich, 2009). The first is that humans are by nature *cognitive misers*. As we mentioned earlier, focused cognitive effort is both slow and can be tiring. We use our autonomous brain to do routine stuff because we would never get anything done otherwise. Imagine having one of those maddening nose itches and having to think "What finger should I use to scratch this and what pressure-to-itch ratio would provide optimal relief?" It is little wonder that many decisions people make are habitual. Of course, not all habits are good and our brief foray into self-defeating behaviours and cognitive biases illustrate times when we would be better off exercising a little more cognitive effort.

The next two causes of Dysrationalia are related to problems with *mindware*, which is a generic label "for the rules, knowledge, procedures, and strategies that a person can retrieve from memory in order to aid decision making and problem solving" (Stanovich, 2013). In relation to Dysrationalia, there are two aspects to mindware…

Firstly, people may not be aware of tools that can help improve their judgement. Paul admits that he never paid much attention during Statistics 101 in high school, yet knowledge of basic probability, statistical, and scientific reasoning has been shown to reduce susceptibility to particular biases. The key point is that these are all bodies of knowledge that have been codified *and can be taught*. The gap in this kind of knowledge is known as the *mindware gap*, and much like cracks in a wall, can be filled with educational "gap filler".

Figure 4.3: Filling the mindware gap

The second mindware problem is much more relevant as it covers much of what this book (and our previous one) is about: *contaminated mindware*. Contaminated mindware runs wide and deep in today's world. It is the world of irrational ideologies, pseudo-science, meme hoaxes and get-rich-quick schemes. If you have spent any time at all on social media, you would have come across posts, tweets, comments and flame-wars arising from contaminated mindware (and in the next chapter, we will show you some more). Unfortunately, unlike the mindware gap, contaminated mindware is much harder to fix because it involves *unlearning* stuff. Going back to the "cracks in the wall" metaphor, it is much easier to fill cracks than to remove filler once it has hardened. Similarly, if cognitive crap has been used to fill mindware gaps, it might never be fully excised. It lingers on, nourished by confirmation bias, remaining every-ready to be operationalised whenever called upon to make an important management decision.

At this point, you might be feeling uncomfortable or apprehensive about being subjected to a rationality test. This is completely understandable and indeed, we confess that we deliberately wrote this section in a way that would play on your sense of ambiguity and bias. We planted seeds of doubt and insecurity by asking loaded questions (How do you feel about having your rationality tested and the scores made public?) and used examples we thought might cause you to think about your own beliefs that others may have labelled irrational (the reference to Paleo diets is bound to have made some readers feel defensive). Our apologies for any offence caused; our intent is merely to show how easy it is to make people feel defensive. It shows how easily System 1 can play havoc with our emotions even when we are engaged in routine activities such as reading a book.

Have no fear though, such an RQ test is a long way away. By Stanovich and West's (2014) own admission, much more work will need to be done:

> "…we are not claiming that there presently exist comprehensive assessment devices for each of these components. Indeed, refining and scaling up many of the small-scale laboratory demonstrations in the literature will be a main task of our future research. Our present claim is only that, in virtually every case, laboratory tasks that have appeared in the published literature give us, at a minimum, a hint at what comprehensive assessment of the particular component would look like" (p. 268).

So rather than be irrational and prejudge how such a test might be used, let's be good cognitive citizens and take a look at the factors Stanovich and West found to be important in determining a person's RQ.

The "Can You Kill James Bond?" Test

The RQ framework for measuring rational thinking is divided into three sections as shown in Figure 4.4 (Stanovich & West, 2014). Don't worry if some of the terms don't make too much sense. Our intent is merely to:

1. Highlight the three broad categories.
2. Ask the question: would testing these areas help improve rational thinking—and by implication, help improve ambiguity intolerance, and reduce the prevalence of self-defeating behaviours and organisational defensive mechanisms that we described in the last two chapters?

Fluid Rationality	Crystallised Rationality	
	Crystallised Facilitators	Crystallised Inhibitors
Resistance to miserly information processing	Probabilistic and statistical reasoning	Belief in paranormal and in intuition
Absence of irrelevant context effects in decision making	Practical numeracy	Value placed on ungrounded knowledge sources
Sensitivity to expected value	Risk knowledge	
Proper knowledge calibration: avoiding overconfidence	Knowledge of scientific reasoning (falsifiability principle)	
Avoidance of myside bias	Financial literacy and economic thinking	Overreliance on introspection
Open minded/objective reasoning styles		Dysfunctional personal beliefs
Prudent attitude toward the future		
Sensitivity to emotions		

Figure 4.4: Components of rationality

Broadly speaking, the fluid rationality column in Figure 4.4 relates to the *thinking dispositions* of the reflective mind. These, if you recall, are the elements that IQ tests do not measure. They include resistance to things such as dogmatism, insensitivity to contradictions, and need for closure. The middle column, *Crystallised Facilitators*, focuses on mindware gaps: those codified and teachable skills that have been shown to improve judgement and reduce one's propensity for bias. As an example, Stanovich (2010, p. 224) cited the *principle of falsifiability*[21] that underpins the scientific method as providing a "wonderful inoculation against many kinds of non-functional beliefs. It is a tool of immense generality." (We'll stress test that assertion in the next chapter).

The right column, *Crystallised Inhibitors*, refers to contaminated mindware (i.e. factors that inhibit rational thinking and undermine judgement). When looking at these, keep in mind that although not all beliefs are true or helpful, the attributes of "truth" and "helpfulness" also have subjective elements. In other words, one person's truth might not be acceptable to another, and the same is true for helpfulness. This implies it is far from easy to make people aware of potential inhibitors because they may not accept the premises on which their beliefs are challenged. This is an area we'll touch upon in Chapter 7.

Stanovich and West (2014) emphasised that the conceptual components in the framework have been extensively researched. After all, Kahneman and Tversky received a Nobel Prize for their voluminous and influential work in this area.

> "unlike many such lists of thinking skills in textbooks, the conceptual components of the fluid characteristics and crystallized knowledge bases listed ... are each grounded in established paradigms of cognitive science. That is, they are not just potentially measurable but in

---

[21] Stanovich (2012) describes the falsifiability principle as thus: "The falsifiability criterion states that, for a theory to be useful, the predictions drawn from it must be specific. The theory must go out on a limb, so to speak, because in telling us what should happen, the theory must also imply that certain things will not happen. If these latter things do happen, then we have a clear signal that something is wrong with the theory: It may need to be modified, or we may

fact have been operationalized and measured at least once in the scientific literature—and in many cases, they have generated enormous empirical literatures" (p. 267).

In fact, The Swedish Academy of Sciences (the folks who hand out the Nobel prizes) stated that Kahneman and Tversky's work was so influential because it spoke to *deep issues concerning human rationality*. Indeed, the Nobel announcement noted that Kahneman and Tversky "discovered how judgement under uncertainty *systematically departs from the kind of rationality* postulated in traditional economic theory" (Kahneman & Smith, 2002).

After examining cognitive miserliness, missing and corrupt mindware in more detail, we feel that an RQ tool could be a very useful diagnostic in a number of ways. But if you are like us, you might be feeling a sense of lingering unease that you can't quite name. Let's see if we can name it by highlighting some things that an RQ tool might need to factor in as it makes the transition from academic prototype to real world supermodel.

To do this we need begin with a story...

Flicking mind-switches

In 2010, Paul, his wife Terrie and two colleagues travelled from Australia to the US to attend a Dialogue Mapping workshop with Jeff Conklin of Cognexus Institute in California. For the purposes of this story, we do not need to go into Dialogue Mapping except to say it is a facilitation technique, designed to help groups deal with complex, messy problems (Conklin, 2005, Culmsee & Awati, 2013).

---

need to look for an entirely new theory. Either way, we shall end up with a theory that is nearer to the truth. In contrast, if a theory does not rule out any possible observations, then the theory can never be changed, and we are frozen into our current way of thinking, with no possibility of progress. Thus a successful theory is not one that accounts for every possible happening because such a theory robs itself of any predictive power."

By this time, Paul was already an experienced practitioner and was attending in a supporting capacity. Even though the class was in the US, the majority of attendees were Australian. Although they were not experienced practitioners, they had all read Jeff's excellent book (Conklin, 2005) and were familiar with his ideas about the nature of complex problems and how one could leverage collective wisdom in such situations. Aside from Conklin, another facilitator and practitioner (also American) was present.

Given this description, you might expect that a good many of the attendees and facilitators had the *right* kind of mindware that Stanovich and West described ... and for the first day and a half of the class, you would be right. Rich conversations took place, ideas were exchanged, insights gleaned and shared learning occurred as a consequence.

The final session of the course was an activity where each person took a turn at facilitating. The way the activity worked was that someone would suggest a topic which the group would then discuss (pretending to be a think-tank or a management team), with the facilitator serving as the conversation mapper and moderator.

Things were going swimmingly: each person took their turn and gained practical experience of facilitating a conversation using Conklin's techniques. Then it was Paul's ("Mr I'm no longer a student") turn to facilitate. It was Paul's wife, Terrie, whose turn it was to pick a topic, and in complete innocence she asked the following question.

> "Well, as a former nurse, I have an interest in healthcare,
> so would like to understand the US healthcare system:
> What does the US healthcare system look like?"

Now another critical piece of context with this story is that by sheer coincidence, this workshop happened just around the time the Affordable Care Act was signed into law. This act—commonly (and pejoratively) referred to as ObamaCare—was the most significant regulatory overhaul of the U.S. healthcare system since 1965, and is still the subject of controversy. Of course, Terrie had little idea of any of this. As an Australian citizen, she was not overly interested in US politics and did not follow it. But what happened for the next 10 minutes was a brilliant example of the role of emotion in reasoning.

Paul, who is experienced in this method of facilitation, was completely unable to rein in the conversation that ensued. This was because the two American attendees were philosophically on different sides of the debate, and *immediately disagreed on facts*. It is important to mention that one of the interlocutors was the highly experienced facilitator mentioned earlier. To the rest of participants (all Australian, with no particular interest in the issue), it seemed like a switch had been flicked in the heads of the two Americans. All the rich discussion of the previous day and a half was replaced by a point and counter-point mode of conversation that went back and forth between two participants who fundamentally disagreed with the basis of each-others answers to the "what are the facts…" question.

Despite Paul's strenuous attempts to rein the exchange in, which included stopping the conversation and trying to take a different tack, he was unable to de-escalate the situation; the conversation always reverted to "argument mode". Conklin allowed this to continue for a while and then finally called time-out. It was at this point the mental switches of the arguing participants flicked back to "rational" mode. The irony of the situation was not lost on the two participants and their "good" mindware kicked in again. The incident provided a unique opportunity for some reflection, an opportunity that Conklin ensured was well taken by all.

The facilitator who was on one side of the argument stated that she had an incredible urge to correct statements she felt were wrong, and in the heat of the conversation was temporarily blinded to the escalation that was happening. When Conklin asked Paul how it felt trying to facilitate in those conditions, despite being an experienced practitioner, he said that he found it impossible to facilitate any meaningful dialogue at all. Conklin then asked the Australian participants what they noticed. Terrie, apart from feeling bad that she had thrown a grenade without knowing, noted how quickly participants moved from a rational, reflective conversation to attack/counterattack.

The experience was a great illustration of how certain conditions can give rise to certain behaviours. Probably the best summary of what transpired came from one participant who wryly stated:

"Well, we may as well talk about abortion now since we just did the second most controversial topic in America!"

Challenges for testing RQ

The story above is a good illustration of the effortlessness with which System 1 thinking can kick in and dominate System 2. It also highlights a couple of other points...

Most people do not perform particularly well in generic human bias tests and one explanation offered for this by researchers is participants are *under-motivated* to allocate the necessary cognitive effort to solving the questions when they do not have a stake in the answer (Klein, 1999). In other words, a generic test for the cognitive miser effect is itself subject to the cognitive miser effect! The difference becomes especially apparent in real-life situations involving judgement, which are very different to the artificial questions or hypothetical situations described in tests such as choosing from two different ball-filled urns.

Yet in the story we just examined, something else happened too. Participants had such strong and passionate opinions on the topic that they never got past System 1. Defensive behaviours kicked in immediately, crowding out more reflective, rational thinking. Remember that this was a *simulated* scenario in a workshop where the entire point was to learn facilitation skills that help groups deal with complex problems. Even so, when a hot button topic was raised, participants became living examples of some of the "problematic individuals" they would likely encounter in their future experiences as facilitators.

Given these issues, three immediate challenges for the RQ test are a) how to account for cognitive miserliness when the test is uninteresting or has no relevance to the participant's personal aims; b) whether one's RQ score makes a difference based on the environment or conditions present when the test is taken; and c) how to account for defensive behaviours when the topic is a contentious one.

To complicate matters further, some researchers have found that the wording of test questions matters significantly when testing for the same bias. Put another way, differently worded tests can yield different results (Aczel, Bago, Szollosi, Foldes, & Lukacs, 2015). If a question truly tests the bias it intended to, there should be no significant difference between results obtained from two different wordings of the same question—particularly if the new wording chosen has already been used in literature to test for that same bias! The lack of consistency in results when questions are reworded might imply that something else is being measured, not just the bias intended. This raises questions about what is actually being measured and by implication, the overall reliability when such scores are aggregated into an RQ.

All this goes to show that a reliable RQ test is probably a long way away.

The difficulty seems to be that it is easier to identify and test individual biases than it is to work out the causal relationships between them. Unfortunately, the latter is necessary for a comprehensive model of rational judgement. The problem of working out causal relationships in detail is a common one in the social and management sciences. In the next chapter, we'll meet someone who faced a similar challenge when trying to determine the factors that make a great team.

Beyond cause and effect

These problems lead us to another longstanding argument about quantitative vs qualitative knowledge. We are taught to believe that quantitative knowledge is superior to qualitative knowledge. Considering our examination of cognitive biases, defensive behaviours and thinking dispositions, it is understandable why it is reasonable to think so. However, it is important to keep in mind what we have learnt about ambiguity tolerance and fetishes. In ambiguous situations, quantification can serve as a *coping* mechanism. In other words, it can become a fetish or security blanket—especially if ones thinking disposition is "just give me the facts" oriented. This is especially dangerous because many complex problems are impossible to characterise quantitatively because facts are scarce, and those available are either ambiguous or disputed.

Nicholas Taleb (2012) noted that such problems require us to go beyond traditional methods that assume the relationships between causes and effects are quantifiable or determinable. He termed these methods as fragile because they fall apart in situations in which uncertainties are hard to quantify ... which pretty much is the case for most important business decisions (in fact, all business decisions excepting purely operational ones). He scathingly called those who believe that all problems can be formulated in terms of unambiguous cause-effect relationships upfront as "fragilistas". In his words:

> "The fragilista falls for the Soviet-Harvard delusion, the (unscientific) overestimation of the reach of scientific knowledge. Because of such delusion, he is what is called a naïve rationalist, a rationalizer, or sometimes just a rationalist, in the sense that he believes that the reasons behind things are automatically accessible to him" (p. 9).

This begs the question as to how one can make business (or any other) decisions in complex situations. Such decisions are invariably ambiguity-ridden because the underlying facts are contested. Clearly, a decision making process that recognises and addresses ambiguity is more likely to succeed than one that doesn't.

However, it's all very well and easy to put the onus for ambiguity tolerance on formulators and implementers. Indeed, many organisations say they encourage "risk taking" and "out-of-the-box thinking", but do nothing to create an environment that fosters these desirable qualities. The point is that behaviours and attitudes at work depend crucially on how comfortable employees feel about taking calculated risks or airing their "crazy" ideas. Based on our collective experience, we'd go out on a limb and say that a significant number of organisations that claim to encourage these qualities do not do enough to create the environment in which they can take root. We suspect this is not so much out of deliberate action or inaction, but a lack of awareness of the influence of conditions (environment) on causes (behaviours).

Finally, as Taleb pointed out in the passage quoted above, it is not possible to rely exclusively on the standard scientific problem solving method when one is dealing with ambiguity-laden issues. The scientific method requires unambiguous facts upfront, or, at the very least, unambiguous (and universally accepted) ways of finding them. The difficulty in ambiguous situations is that the "facts", such as they are, are open to interpretation. Worse, it is often not clear as to how one should go about finding "reliable facts". Differences of opinion regarding these points can deal a knockout blow to the scientific method—stop it cold in its tracks. The point is, the process of establishing the facts is a far from straightforward one when different parties hold different opinions on what's important and what's not … and one cannot make progress on solving the underlying problem until that's sorted out to everyone's satisfaction. We'd go so far as to say this is the single biggest problem facing organisations today. Much of what we see—including the fetishised over-reliance on canned processes, strategies and methodologies—stems from a failure to appreciate this point.

In the next chapter, we use a number of examples to illustrate and amplify the importance of conditions and their importance in getting the right facts and the facts right.

5

Causes, Conditions and the Replication Crisis

Sheldon: I'm having some difficulty bonding with a colleague at work, so I'm doing a little research to better understand why my current friends like me.

Penny: Yes, well, that is a good question. But is this really the best way to figure it out?

Sheldon: I agree. The social sciences are largely hokum. But short of putting electrodes in your brain and monitoring your response to my companionship, this is the best I can do.

Penny: Okay, question one: "Rank the following aspects of Sheldon Cooper in order of appeal: intelligence, ruthless attention to hygiene, playfulness, Java applet writing?"

Sheldon: I know. I may have started off with a fairly obvious one. An aspect of my most appealing trait—playfulness. Why don't you just go ahead and rank that number one? I'm afraid you're on your own for the rest. It should take you no more than three hours.

Penny: Well, wait, how many questions are on this thing?

Sheldon: Only two hundred and eleven. Don't worry. In deference to you, I've kept them all at a high school graduate reading level.

Penny: [sarcastically] Thanks, pal.

Sheldon: You got it, buddy.

Penny: Sheldon, honey, did you ever consider making friends by being … I don't know … pleasant?

Sheldon: Well, that's certainly a thought-provoking hypothesis. May I suggest it as the topic for your essay?

Physics envy

If all of the various sciences were WWE wrestlers or MMA fighters, the undisputed world heavyweight champion would have to be physics. Like a championship fighter, physics makes big, bold claims but then backs it up in the ring with a combination of strength and razor sharp precision. This is reflected in the models that physicists produce: models that can be so consistent with what is measured and observed that they transcend supermodel status and become *laws*. The difference between a law and a supermodel is that not only are laws good looking (in a nerdy mathematical way), they have also been legitimised via extensive empirical testing and observation. It is precisely such validation that enables rocket scientists to use Newton's Law of Gravitation with full confidence that it will work. Our ability to put satellites into orbit around Mars assures us their trust isn't misplaced.

Physics hangs out with several other well-regarded science heavyweights, collectively known as the natural sciences. In the knowledge hierarchy, the natural sciences are at the top of the heap. Within the various branches and sub-branches of the natural sciences, Chemistry would be the number one challenger for heavyweight title held by physics, simply by virtue of the fact that it has many supermodels and laws of its own. Biology and Geology, while still in the cool-kids club, do not have as many precise laws and are therefore not as revered as physics. In general, it seems the more quantitative a discipline, the more likely it is to be considered a heavyweight.

After the natural sciences come the social sciences, such as economics, political science, psychology and management science. These disciplines would dearly love to be held in the same esteem as physics, but are much further down the pecking order and have a *massive* inferiority complex about it.

For many, physics exemplifies the gold standard of precision and rigour that all disciplines ought to aspire to. Consequently, those working in "softer" disciplines (a pejorative term that is sometimes used by physicists and quantitative folks to describe qualitative fields) feel pressured to formulate laws that have the same level of technical sophistication and accuracy as those created by physicists. Economists for example, have long sought to identify a deterministic "natural law" of markets in the same way physicists have discovered natural laws for gravity and electromagnetism. The story is much the same in psychology and management science—and it is easy to understand why. Imagine for example, the usefulness of a mathematical model for getting the best out of teams and individuals, or for perfect leadership, or an optimal business strategy. If such natural or fundamental laws could be identified, we would be able to make better decisions and take immediate action, without having to go through the pain and trouble of convincing others before doing so (after all, a law can't be wrong, right?).

The need to obtain precise mathematical expressions of fundamental concepts among softer sciences is often referred to as *physics envy* by some. Unfortunately, while the other sciences are not short of ideas and models, there are few that are as general or accurate as physical laws. In some social science branches, such as economics and psychology, none have emerged at all—at least none a physicist like Dr Sheldon Cooper would take seriously.

There is a good reason for this: a key difference between physics and social sciences is that the former deals with the inanimate world, whereas the latter deals with humans who have minds of their own. With the knowledge afforded by laws of physics, it is possible to manipulate inanimate objects with great precision—getting the New Horizons mission to far flung Pluto is a brilliant testament to our ability to do so. However, it is well-nigh impossible to manipulate living things (let alone humans) with a similar degree of precision as they tend to behave in unpredictable ways, often for no apparent reason at all. As a result, the relationship between cause and effect, which is clear cut in physics, is considerably more tenuous in the social sciences. In fact, for all of Isaac Newton's contributions to physics, he nevertheless lost a considerable chunk of his fortune in a 17th century equivalent of the dotcom bust and is said to have remarked, "I can calculate the motions of the heavenly bodies, but not the madness of people." (We speculate that he may have benefited from a Stanovich RQ test).

Fast forward three hundred-something years and you have renowned physicist Richard Feynman acknowledging physics' predictability advantage, when he once said, "Imagine how much harder physics would be if electrons had feelings!" Luckily for physicists, the only egos they have to deal with are each other's. Social scientists, on the other hand, not only have to contend with their own egos and those of their colleagues, but also those of the subjects they are studying.

Superficially, though, it all seems fine: social scientists frame hypotheses, construct theories and models just like the hard sciences. As per the scientific method, these are then tested via experiments which others replicate in order to validate them. Insights from this process should result in continual refinement with the eventual emergence of rigorous models that have empirical backing. Such is the pervasiveness of this thinking that a New York Times Article by Kevin Clarke and David Primot (2012), noted that for a time, The American Journal of Political Science explicitly refused to review theoretical models that weren't tested.

So we have lots of theories and lots of results across the social sciences (even political science!) and it seems that social scientists are getting to be just like those awesome physicists that they want to grow up to be. Indeed, many social scientists have spawned supermodels, sold millions of books and graced TED events[22].

But, like a typical horror movie, the veneer of suburban normality is quickly stripped away as the story progresses…

An inconvenient empirical result

A recent set of empirical tests in the field of social psychology has caused considerable angst among some researchers. You can tell something is really controversial in academia when researchers eschew the usual process of academic debate via journals and take to firing broadsides from their blogs instead. Here's the story…

In 2015, the Open Science Collaboration (2015) conducted replications of 100 studies in psychological science. The basic idea in replication is just what the term implies: if you make a scientific claim,

---

[22] https://en.wikipedia.org/wiki/TED_(conference)

others should be able to verify it by following your reasoning, procedures and methods.

As you might imagine, replication is a huge cornerstone of the scientific method. All the results of scientific experiments should be *independently reproducible under the same conditions.* This guards against uncritical acceptance of findings that might be inadvertent false positives, subject to measurement bias ... or just plain wrong.

Rumbles about the lack of replication studies in psychology had been occurring for years, giving rise to accusations that the discipline was not as scientific as it claimed to be. So the attempt to replicate 100 studies was a big deal. Imagine then, the reaction when it was reported that *only 36% of the replicated studies yielded significant findings compared to 97% of the original studies that reported significant effects.* The study concluded by stating:

> "A large portion of replications produced weaker evidence for the original findings despite using materials provided by the original authors, review in advance for methodological fidelity, and high statistical power to detect the original effect sizes. Moreover, correlational evidence is consistent with the conclusion that variation in the strength of initial evidence ... was more predictive of replication success than variation in the characteristics of the teams conducting the research ... The latter factors certainly can influence replication success, but they did not appear to do so here" (p. 943).

Amongst the many who offered their views on the replication issue, Nobel laureate Daniel Kahneman (2014) suggested that researchers who published the original studies should have the right to participate as advisers in the replication of their research. His concern was that these researchers, whose reputations were potentially at risk, may have additional context or knowledge that was not codified in the original method sections of their published works. Another team attempting to replicate the work could miss subtle, yet critical factors which might explain some of the discrepancies between the original and replicated study.

Such a suggestion would seem foreign to a physicist, and downright offensive to science purists. Remember, the essence of the replicability principle in science is that the experiment can be *independently reproduced*. Accordingly, some science types within psychology disagreed with Kahneman's suggestion on the grounds that a) it was not scientific; and b) it treated the symptoms and not the cause. Dr Andrew Wilson, a psychologist from Leeds Metropolitan University, suggested on his blog that if replication problems in psychology are because of unclear or vague method sections, then the obvious solution is to publish more detailed method sections to make it clear for any aspiring replicator.

> "Here's a crazy alternative solution: how about we psychologists all agree to write Methods sections that would pass a first year Research Methods course and include all relevant information required for replication? ... If you can't stand the replication heat, get out of the empirical kitchen because publishing your work means you think it's ready for prime time, and if other people can't make it work based on your published methods then that's your problem and not theirs" (Wilson, 2014).

Ouch!

A pivotal issue in the debate is that the replication principle states that experimental results are expected to be the same *under the same conditions*. Once you move from inanimate objects into the world of conscious entities that can alter their behaviour, it gets considerably harder to ensure the same conditions. In an article entitled "Psychology Is Not in Crisis", Lisa Feldman Barrett (2015) stated:

> "Does this mean that the phenomenon in question is necessarily illusory? Absolutely not. If the studies were well designed and executed, it is more likely that the phenomenon from Study A is true only under certain conditions. The scientist's job now is to figure out what

those conditions are, in order to form new and better hypotheses to test."

This sounds entirely plausible and consistent with the principle of replicability, until you consider that: a) very few replication studies in psychology were being accepted for publication until this issue came to light (which is somewhat ironic given what psychology has taught us about the numerous forms of bias); and b) Stanovich might call this logic *irrational* because such arguments risk making scientific claims *unfalsifiable*, which was one of the examples of a mindware gap that we examined in the last chapter.

We suspect Stanovich cites lack of falsifiability as a mindware gap because of what it permits. Think about it … this is the same logic a conspiracy theorist might use when they refute iron-clad counter evidence by stating "Well, that's what they want you to think." Put simply, this approach provides a conceptual escape clause by allowing for another as-yet-unknown variable or factor that could account for the difference between reality and the theory in question. Philosopher Stephen Law (2011), in his book "Believing Bullshit", called this *moving the semantic goalposts*. This, for most ardent proponents of the scientific method, is a slippery slope. How can one refute dodgy theories if their proponents keep adding new variables to them to keep them alive? Come to think of it, this is exactly what the "Five Stages of Bullshit Legitimation" model presented in Chapter 2 does too!

The cost of selective physics envy

There are instances of high-visibility claims made in the social sciences that were shown up to be questionable later, but not before costing billions of dollars and impacting the livelihoods of millions of people for the worse. In the first chapter, we examined the story of the flawed work that underpinned the rationale for applying austerity measures. If you recall, apart from researchers cherry-picking the data they worked with, their Excel spreadsheet had an elementary error in it. In this case, the replication effort that exposed the flaw came too late for the citizens of affected countries. The lesson here for policymakers is fairly obvious: don't rely on one model, no matter how sexy and authoritative it appears—and don't forget to check that damned spreadsheet!

The Austerity example is not the first time a flawed model has been relied on by policymakers, and it is a pretty sure bet that it won't be the last. Indeed, there's a similar example from finance that occurred a few years ago. In this case the story begins with a paper published in 2000 that had a formula with the same seductive power of Einstein's famous one—but for Wall Street bankers rather than physicists. In case you're curious, here it is:

$$C_\rho(u, v) = \Phi_\rho(\Phi^{-1}(u), \Phi^{-1}(v))$$

If you're like us, this formula will probably make little sense to you. That's OK ... many in the finance sector who adopted it enthusiastically didn't understand it either. Their lack of understanding of the assumptions and applicability of this formula is one of the things that contributed to the super-mess known as the global financial crisis (GFC) of 2007/2008.

The GFC is a complex, multilayered beast, deserving its own book, so we will briefly cover only the part in which this model played a role.

In the good old days (aka last century), when a bank granted a loan or mortgage, they would hold it to maturity. A consequence of this was if the mortgage holder defaulted on the loan, the bank would make a loss. Therefore, banks were careful who they lent money to, and they commonly would sell their mortgages to someone else (in financial parlance, they would *securitize* it). This meant that while the bank would forego the interest payments, they would still collect fees for selling the mortgage and have the added benefit of reducing their direct risk because the other party would carry the exposure. Not a bad deal considering you eliminate risk and collect a fee while doing so.

Given that many loans were on-sold in this way, banks started getting creative. Since many people spread risk by investing in managed funds instead of directly buying stocks in the market, banks began to package different securities together into new products called packaged debt securities. Agencies like Moodys would then assess these packaged securities and give them a rating to help investors to make a more informed decision about whether to invest in them.

The stage was set for the entry of the magic formula. This supermodel, formulated by David Li (2000), provided a quick and mathematically elegant way to model the relationship between the individual debt securities in a package. In essence, the formula spits out a probability of the securities going bad all at once. Using this model, banks were able to quickly calculate a precise risk score for packaged debt securities. This was a big deal because the old approach was to manually sort through the historical data on actual defaults, which not only took ages, it was also pretty tedious and painstaking work to boot.

Credit agencies, which investors relied on for risk ratings, were equally seduced by the promise of physics-like mathematical precision. Previously, they assessed the risk of these packaged debts based on the much less cool approach used by funds managers called *diversification*: ensuring (often manually) that different types of assets like subprime debt, business loans, student loans, and credit card debts made up the mix. Li's model was seen as a more accurate, scientific and efficient way to do it. Such was the pervasiveness of this model, that it was even enshrined in regulatory frameworks that were used to determine how much capital banks needed when they had packaged debt securities on their books. In other words, regulators used the same supermodel when they assessed the assets banks needed to cover their liabilities.

As you might imagine, a lot rode on that formula. Indeed, with that level of pervasiveness, it is easy to see why some might have considered it a *law* of finance. Perhaps it is precisely this kind of thinking that caused the market for packaged debt securities to reach breathless heights. In 2000, when Li published his influential article, the market was less than $70 billion US dollars. In 2007, it was $500 billion per year.

Unfortunately, like all models this one has its limitations too. Unlike our austerity example though, there were no spreadsheet errors (Li is a PhD statistician), but nevertheless, doubts and concerns regarding its *assumptions* were raised by researchers as early as 2001 (Frey, McNeil, & Nyfeler, 2001). One key concern was the model seemed to fit reality under "typical credit conditions" but appeared to understate the likelihood of "extreme portfolio loss events". Another criticism, one that Li acknowledged, was an assumption that the relationship between all of the securities in the package remained constant. In a 2009 Forbes article, Susan Lee called this "hilariously silly":

> "In the financial world, relationships between, and among, assets are extremely fluid. Abiding by one number is akin to spotting a fish in a swiftly moving stream and going back an hour later to catch it" (Lee, 2009).

By 2008, an "extreme portfolio loss event" happened in the form of the subprime mortgage meltdown where a cooling property market, rising interest rates, and risky loans to people who could barely afford them began to bite. At this point, the once beautiful model fell apart because the conditions changed and financial markets began behaving in ways that the model did not cater for. Packaged securities previously rated Triple-A by agencies were worthless and investors in them lost everything.

No-one quite knows how much the financial crisis cost, but a 2012 report by Better Markets (2012) conservatively estimated it to be around $12.8 trillion dollars. While this cannot be blamed on a single formula, its use contributed to a scenario where significant risks went unnoticed.

In this example, the issue was less about replication, and more about the questionable assumptions behind the model. The apparent mathematical simplicity and elegance of the formula, combined with its alleged applicability to complex, real-world scenarios made it highly popular—so popular it became a supermodel. Exactly as in the case of the austerity example, those seduced by it were oblivious to its flaws, despite researchers having pointed them out much earlier.

The result was a very expensive lesson in the practical applicability of quantitative financial models, one for which the world is still paying the price.

Although quants (finance speak for "math geeks") employ the mathematical approaches and techniques of physics, the entities they deal with are fundamentally different. To emphasise a point we've already made, planets (and electrons) have no free will, so physicists can build models of them with the assurance they will continue to orbit stars (and nuclei). On the other hand, financial models, despite their mathematical sophistication, provide a very simplified picture of reality. In the financial universe, what we observe is governed by the behaviour of individuals who, as we've learnt in the last two chapters, are not consistent in their behaviour. A fundamental assumption of economics is that people make decisions on a rational basis. This assumption has been questioned many times over, and proven to be incorrect in many situations, particularly those in which the underlying fundamentals change.

The lesson for the finance industry and the rest of us is obvious: *stress test the model*. Change the underlying assumptions in the model and see what pops out the other end. Test models using historical data that covers extreme events to see if assumptions hold up. Had the various players in the financial risk management process—banks, regulators and ratings agencies—done this, the likelihood of the GFC being as severe as it was might have been significantly reduced.

The cost of complete physics envy...

By this point, some of our readers may be thinking that social sciences' penchant for superficially beautiful (but essentially unverifiable) models is a major problem. Some may take Sheldon Cooper's view that "the social sciences are largely hokum." An even greater number might think: "These authors are painting a one-sided picture and are cherry picking case studies to support their view." We absolutely agree with the last group: we have been messing with you to see if your System 1 defences kicked in. If they did, all we can say is "Haha … got you!" We are not apologising this time. You should've been expecting it by now … but there is another side to all this.

Let's now flip this argument totally on its head. There is an important (no, urgent!) problem that has been modelled in various ways that have been validated using multiple, independent data sets (that is, the work has replicated). Yet, a significant portion of the general public remains sceptical about the conclusions. You may have guessed that we're referring to the increasing gap between scientific evidence for the causes of climate change and the public acceptance of those findings. As we will illustrate, this is a great example of how physics envy (and well-meaning scientists) can be manipulated by those who are motivated to discredit science and scientists.

A study in 2015 (Capstick, Whitmarsh, Poortinga, Pidgeon, & Upham) examined trends in climate change and found that sections of the public appeared to have lost faith in climate science and climate scientists—especially since the late 2000s. Yet a major study of scientific consensus on climate change (Cook, et al., 2013) found that when *multiple methods* were used to estimate the degree of scientific consensus about human-caused climate change, 97% or more of climate scientists were convinced it was happening (we emphasised "multiple methods" to highlight the replicability principle).

However, as reported in the October 2015 update of the "Climate Change in the American Mind" survey (Leiserowitz, Maibach, Roser-Renouf, Feinberg, & Rosenthal), only 53% of American adults agreed and only 10% were aware that nearly all climate scientists agree human-caused global warming is happening. Furthermore, only 4% reported having changed their opinion about global warming in the prior year. We are not just picking on the US either. Maibach, Myers, & Leiserowitz (2014) reported a multi-country poll showing similar results when people were asked if they believed a majority of scientists agreed the problem was urgent and enough was known to take action. These were Russia (23%), Indonesia (33%), Japan (43%), Brazil (44%), India (48%), and Mexico (48%).

A plethora of explanations have been proposed for the recent divergence of opinion, so many that a discussion of them could fill an entire book. One very successful method, pioneered by the tobacco industry, is to *manipulate ambiguity intolerance and physics envy.* This works by setting the expectation that scientists must deliver hard facts and conclusions with 100% certainty and then exploiting the fact that it is impossible to do so. Perverse logic right? But it worked a treat…

The subtle art of contaminating mindware

The tobacco industry's longstanding tactic of manipulating ambiguity was exposed in a famous 1963 memo that was stolen, along with many other documents, from a law firm that represented tobacco company Brown & Williamson. The memo, made public in 1994, indicated that top executives in the tobacco industry knew about the dangers of smoking back in the early 1960s. More important, it provides a fascinating glimpse into the tactics employed by the industry to keep the debate about the facts alive. Here is one of the many juicy direct quotes from it:

> "Doubt is our product since it is the best means of competing with the 'body of fact' that exists in the mind of the general public. It is also the means of establishing a controversy. If we are successful in establishing a controversy at the public level, then there is an opportunity to put across the real facts about smoking and health. Doubt is also the limit of our 'product.' Unfortunately, we cannot take a position directly opposing the anti-cigarette forces and say that cigarettes are a contributor to good health. No information that we have supports such a claim" (Smoking and Health Proposal, 1969).

This use of ambiguity to challenge science exploits the very basis of the scientific method and as such, is a highly effective method to manufacture doubt about established facts. By the mid-1980s, tobacco companies had perfected the approach to the extent that one company had developed a "discredit the product" template that people could fill in when a new threat arose[23]. This template, illustrated in Figure 5.1, included items such as:

- **Situation:** What needs to be discredited.
- **Risk Assessment** (low, moderate or high).
- **Strategy**: How to go about discrediting the threat.
- **Action Plan**: Tasks, timeframes and accountabilities for getting it done.

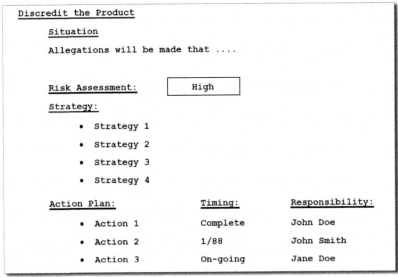

Figure 5.1: The "Discredit the Product" template used by the tobacco industry, adapted from (McKenna, 1988)

By 1993, a 254-page manual called "Bad Science: A Resource Book" was circulated. This document was used to refute issues around second hand smoke, and listed key messages to continually push home, including:

---

[23] This material is available online. Go to
https://industrydocuments.library.ucsf.edu/ and search for the word "discredit"

- "Too often, science is manipulated to fulfil a political agenda."
- "Government agencies, too often, betray the public trust by violating principles of good science in a desire to achieve a political goal."
- "No agency is more guilty of adjusting science to support preconceived public policy prescriptions than the Environmental Protection Authority."
- "Public policy decisions that are based on bad science impose enormous economic costs on all aspects of society."
- "Proposals that seek to improve indoor air quality by singling out tobacco smoke only enable bad science to become a poor excuse for enacting new laws and jeopardising individual liberties."

Each of the above points were backed up with supporting material that included lots of quotes and a selection of articles from various sources that supported each point. Thus proponents were well armed with multiple messages of doubt, and backed them up with lots of references, *just like an article in a scientific journal.* Confronted with such seemingly authoritative information, how on earth could lay people (journalists included) tell fact from fiction?

In Stanovich's terms, the tobacco industry gave us a textbook lesson on how physics envy can be manipulated to create contaminated mindware.

It is important to note that while the tobacco industry was eventually exposed and these tactics laid bare, it took insider exposure rather than scientific evidence to nail the coffin. The key point we want to emphasise is that *the scientific method by itself is not enough for problems in which doubt can be easily manufactured.* One has to resort to other tactics to gain mindshare. Indeed, the arguments over climate science provide yet another illustration of this point.

Consider this leaked memo written in 2002 by US political consultant, Frank Luntz for then president George W Bush. It clearly stated the strategic value of uncertainty:

> "Should the public come to believe that the scientific issues are settled, their views about global warming will change accordingly. Therefore, you need to continue to make the lack of scientific certainty a primary issue in the debate" (Luntz, 2003).

After all, the lobbyist asks, you wouldn't get on a plane if you were only 97% certain of landing safely, would you? Given this, surely it is reasonable that people are unwilling to board the "climate change is caused by humans" plane. Not so, says climate scientist Richard Nelson (2015), because there will never be 100% certainty.

> "What I want to emphasize here is that whereas the general knowledge about climate change and its causes is strong, specific knowledge about future effects and their timing is not only weak, but inevitably so. But the expectation that climate science should be like physics has fostered the expectation that the research should provide physics-like precision and accuracy. These false expectations lead to an inappropriate attention—by scientists, policymakers, and the interested public alike—to questions of uncertainty that are unlikely ever to be resolved because of the nature of the phenomena being studied."

The absurdity of physics envy

By this point, you might be thinking your authors are a pair of schizophrenics. We started by arguing that more physics envy is needed in social psychology and then argued that it was a zero sum game because it is easily manipulated by creating doubt. One might conclude that it's about time physics is taken down a rung or two down the ladder. Luckily for us, that's not too hard because, as it happens, physics—the undisputed heavyweight champion of rationality and accuracy—is itself subject to physics envy!

One of the goals of physics is to find the fundamental constituents of matter. The history of the effort is essentially a story of how physicists hypothesised smaller and smaller entities, starting from the atom to protons and electrons, to quarks and to the present day speculations on string theory[24]. To verify the existence of these hypothesised entities, experimental physicists have to break down matter by throwing high-energy particles at it and examine the resulting fragments for evidence of the entities. The best known experimental apparatus for doing this is CERN's Large Hadron Collider (LHC), where the Higgs Boson (aka the God Particle) was discovered.

The LHC can generate particle beams with very high energies, but it has its limits. The problem is many of the entities proposed by theoretical physicists (strings being one of them) require energies higher than the LHC can produce. As a result, many present-day theoretical results in fundamental physics are essentially untestable with the current state of art.

More to the point, while these theories have the sort of mathematical elegance and explanatory power that give physics its esteemed status at the top of the science heap, *it may well be impossible to experimentally verify such theories in the future*. This stems from the fact that we are approaching fundamental limits of nature and may not be able to go much further. Moreover, there is a limit of a more practical kind: peering deeper into the fundamental structure of nature would require a machine considerably more powerful than the LHC. The cost of building such a machine would be astronomical, and likely unjustifiable in view of the myriad of pressing problems faced by humanity today. The upshot of all this is that theoretical constructs as string theory, supersymmetry, and multiple universes *might not be falsifiable*, and if you subscribe to Stanovich's ideas, might not be rational either.

Perhaps, as a result of the above, some theoretical physicists have suggested a change in how theories should be judged. They propose that if a model is sufficiently elegant and explanatory, *it need not be tested experimentally to be accepted*.

---

[24] See https://en.wikipedia.org/wiki/String_theory for more.

Now, if you think the infighting between social psychologists around replicability and the scientific method was bad, imagine how this argument goes down in the very discipline that has most benefited from replicability and the scientific method! To that end, in December 2014 two physicists launched a salvo in the journal Nature, declaring this issue *a battle for the heart and soul of physics*. They defended the scientific method and reiterated that a theory must be falsifiable to be scientific. The elegance and explanatory power of a model is all well and good, but does *not* exempt it from experimental verification.

> "These unprovable hypotheses are quite different from those that relate directly to the real world and that are testable through observations—such as the standard model of particle physics and the existence of dark matter and dark energy. As we see it, theoretical physics risks becoming a no-man's-land between mathematics, physics and philosophy that does not truly meet the requirements of any" (Ellis & Silk, 2014).

One of the key concerns of the authors is the potential damage to the reputation of science in areas such as climate change where there is a widening gap between scientific and public opinion. They claim that it is only by ensuring testability *across the board* can science defend itself from attacks on its credibility. If one makes exemptions, a lay person could legitimately ask, "If you can't *prove* that string theory explains everything, how can you prove that humans are responsible for climate change?"

> "To state that a theory is so good that its existence supplants the need for data and testing in our opinion risks misleading students and the public as to how science should be done and could open the door for pseudoscientists to claim that their ideas meet similar requirements."

When you consider our journey through beautiful yet deeply flawed supermodels, cognitive seesaw kids, ambiguity, social defences, cognitive biases, contaminated mindware, and the manipulation of doubt, we can understand where these physicists are coming from. But consider the counter argument: when we reach the limits (both technological and fundamental) of our ability to test phenomena, should we preclude more elegant, explanatory theories only because we have no way to empirically test them?

> "How are we to determine whether a theory is true if it cannot be validated experimentally? Should we abandon it just because, at a given level of technological capacity, empirical support might be impossible? If not, how long should we wait for such experimental machinery before moving on: ten years? Fifty years? Centuries?" (Frank & Glieser, 2015).

Another way to look at the issue is to imagine that Albert Einstein did not actually develop his theories, but it was actually his distant ancestor, Bob Einstein. In the 1700s, Bob worked out the relativity theories and the supporting math, but had no way to empirically test them because of the primitive technology of the time. He was deemed a crackpot and his ideas were not considered science. Several hundred years later, Albert found his ancestor's theory, and with the advent of technology, was able to test it. Although this is just a thought experiment, there are cases of proponents of theories being ridiculed and hounded by the scientific establishment, only to be proven correct later[25]. The question remains though: if falsifiability is not a sufficient criterion for determining "scientific-ness", what is?

---

[25] Two names that come to mind are Georg Cantor (https://goo.gl/D7ZalC) and Ludwig Boltzmann (https://goo.gl/OtzSHH). The former was a mathematician who invented the theory of transfinite numbers (the idea that there are different kinds of infinities, some being larger than others) and the latter, a physicist who was one of the early champions of the notion that all matter is made up of atoms and molecules

The complexity of conditions...

Taking stock of the topics we have traversed, we notice a common theme (and no—it's not that science is just as messed up as the typical organisation). We began with physics envy: the predisposition of practitioners of so-called softer disciplines to aspire to the mathematical rigor and certainty of quantitative modelling. Our neuroscience-informed discussions on ambiguity tolerance in Chapter 3 sheds light on why such models are so seductive: the clear cause-effect relationships embodied in such models serve to reduce ambiguity by reducing cognitive dissonance—i.e. they *feel* right.

We then explored the replication problem in social psychology, which tells us that reproducibility of studies that test such cause-effect models is alarmingly low, both in frequency as well as consistency of results. The underlying issue is the *difficulty of reproducing the conditions of the original study.* Indeed, whether the difficulty arises from a bad theory or model, a poorly written methods statement or anything else, the net effect is that *the conditions of the original study are hard (if not impossible) to pin down and therefore, hard to reproduce.*

We then looked at economics where we saw an example of an elegant model that gained legitimacy, and was widely used until the underlying economic conditions changed and caused damage to the tune of 12.8 trillion dollars. Once again, we see the issue of *insufficient appreciation of conditions.* In this case, not fully understanding the conditions under which the assumption of constant relationships between securities holds, leading to a mega-debacle.

We also looked at physics itself, with its own struggles via the debate on whether the scientific method is appropriate given that we may have reached the physical limits of testability. This raises the prospect that we may end up with a lot of Bob Einstein types. When you think about it, this pretty much sums up the predicament of all management authors—ourselves included.

Of course, all of this give lots of juicy ammo to the doubt industry, which has long understood that playing on uncertainty provides an incredibly powerful means to contaminate mindware. Accordingly, they play on ambiguity intolerance and physics envy by suggesting that only when 100% definitive answers can be provided, can we legitimately take action. In the case of the tobacco industry, this tactic worked for 30 years. It came undone in the end, not via the scientific method, but industrial espionage.

Whew! Is your head spinning yet? We are dealing with a heck of a dilemma (or put better, a complex series of interrelated dilemmas with no clear cut answers). In fact, this is what's known as a *wicked problem*—a beast we will talk more about in the next chapter.

From causes to conditions

At this point, it is worth noting that despite being a business book, at no point in this chapter have we cast our physics envy lens onto corporate concerns like project management, human resource management, information management and knowledge management. All you MBA types reading this might think that your discipline gets off scot-free. Not so: our discussion about the importance of conditions (or the environment) now enables us to turn our attention to management science. For reasons that will soon be obvious, we'll begin with the story of Richard Hackman[26].

From the mid 1960s, Hackman spent his career researching team performance, leadership effectiveness, and the design of self-managing teams and organisations. One of his last papers published just prior to his demise was a reflective piece called "From causes to conditions in group research" (Hackman R. , 2012). In this paper, he reflected on his long career including what he later considered to be his mistakes.

Hackman started with the observation that many people tend to attribute the success of a team to the qualities and actions of its leader. Conversely, poor leadership is one of the first reasons offered for poorly performing teams. Hackman thought that the tendency to wrongly assign credit (or blame) for success (or failure) solely to the leader was so pervasive that he labelled it the *Leadership Attribution Error*. He suggested

---

[26] http://hbswk.hbs.edu/item/j-richard-hackman-1940-2013

this attribution error stemmed from people attaching causal significance to things they can see compared to less obvious things that operate in the background.

That said, this observation isn't particularly interesting except that it casts doubt on the industry of leadership consultants, their trademarked models, books and pricey training courses ostensibly aimed at helping leaders learn and execute all of the things that facilitate outstanding team performance. Here it is in Hackman's own words (emphasis ours):

> "Everything I know about leadership courses suggests that, when well executed, attendees absolutely love them. The problem is that research evidence that would document the benefits for team performance claimed by the offerers of such courses is hard to find. *It may be hard to find because it does not exist*" (Hackman R. , 2004).

It gets worse. Early in his career, Hackman spent considerable time examining the factors other than leadership that make teams work really well. He studied many different types of teams, aiming to distil the essential causes of their success or failure. After all, if we can work out fundamental levers or laws that govern team success, then organisations would surely work better because they can start to pull those levers and/or design interventions to apply those laws.

But Hackman found that things were not so simple. Try as he did, he could not *isolate causal factors* that influenced team performance. Indeed, every time he developed a model and tested it via interventions on real teams, *he found that there was no meaningful difference in performance*. He subsequently reviewed the literature and found other researchers had faced the same problem. Referring to this, Hackman wrote (emphasis ours):

> "The title of Kaplan's review article provides a compact summary of his findings: 'The conspicuous absence of evidence that process consultation enhances group performance.' Kaplan also conducted an experimental study in which he found that even a well-conceived and

competently implemented intervention intended to improve the quality of group interaction, although it did foster member satisfaction with the group experience, *actually impaired measured group performance*" (Hackman R. , 2012, p. 432).

The contention of Hackman is that most interventions intended to *improve* a group's performance are not only doomed to fail, but will often result in effects contrary to what was intended.

> "Consider, for example, the track records of exhortation, close monitoring and supervision, and the administration of behavior-contingent rewards or punishments. All these interventions have spotty records at best—they make little or no difference (as is the case for exhorting group members to exhibit better teamwork), or they induce resistance and reactance (in response to close monitoring and supervision), or they require considerable overhead to administer and ensure fairness (as generally is the case for attempts to shape work behavior using operant techniques)" (p. 434).

Thoughtful managers will be well aware of this conundrum. In terms of what we have seen earlier, these well-meaning but flawed interventions are a form of contaminated mindware.

Humans instinctively think in terms of causes and effects. The problem is that in the social sphere it is often difficult to separate causes and effects cleanly. This is exactly what Hackman found in the case of team behaviour: the assumption that causal factors could be isolated from each-other and their effects unambiguously quantified turned out to be wrong. The reality, in case of group behaviour and performance, is that it cannot be analysed in terms of well-defined cause-effect relationships alone.

> "To try to partial out and assess the causal effects of each component can be an exercise in frustration

because each ingredient of what may be a spicy stew loses its zest when studied separately from the others" (p. 440).

This is analogous to an issue with RQ tests we mentioned in the last chapter. Research indicates that differently worded questions designed to test for same cognitive bias, can yield different results. This suggests that these tests are not an objective measure of the bias. Similar considerations led Hackman to realize that instead of trying to isolate causal factors of team performance, it may be more useful to explore *the enabling conditions that give rise to great teams.*

Now if you think there is no difference between causes and conditions, we beg to differ. If you have ever argued with people in your field whether a policy, process, methodology or model is great or completely sucks, eventually someone will say something like "Well it can work for the *right* organisation." The implicit assumption here is that under certain conditions, something that works for one organisation may be a complete disaster for another (thereby causing a problem with the very notion of a "best practice").

In essence, Hackman wanted to know what "right" looked like.

Accordingly, he re-examined and refocused his work in a way that enabled him to examine conditions. Over time, he found six conditions that, when present, led to better team performance. There conditions, if present from an early stage of group formation, had an overwhelmingly positive effect on the performance of the team:

1. **A real team:** Interdependence among members, clear boundaries distinguishing members from non-members and moderate stability of membership over time
2. **A compelling purpose:** A purpose that is clear, challenging, and consequential. It energizes team members and fully engages their talents
3. **Right people:** People who had task expertise, self-organised and skill in working collaboratively with others
4. **Clear norms of conduct:** Team understands clearly what behaviours are, and are not, acceptable.

5. **A supportive organisational context:** The team has the resources it needs and the reward system provides recognition and positive consequences for excellent team performance
6. **Appropriate coaching:** The right sort of coaching for the team was provided at the right time

It is important to note that Hackman did not rate any one of these conditions as being more important than the others. He emphasised that all are needed for teams to have a good chance of being high performing. He also noted that much of the team development work has to be done upfront, rather than through interventionist approaches later. Consider this quote (emphasis ours):

> "Let me go out on a limb and make rough estimates of the size of these effects. I propose that 60 per cent of the difference in how well a group eventually does is determined by the quality of the condition-setting pre-work the leader does. Thirty per cent is determined by how the initial launch of the group goes. *And only 10 per cent is determined by what the leader does after the group is already underway with its work.* This view stands in stark contrast to popular images of group leadership—the conductor waving a baton throughout a musical performance or an athletic coach shouting instructions from the sidelines during a game" (p. 438).

If this is indeed the case, then much of the received wisdom on leadership is misleading if not downright wrong ... but that's not what interests us most about Hackman's conclusions.

So what?

Hackman made the point that people tend to attribute team performance to the leader. Similarly, people commonly attribute success or failure in problem solving to the methods, processes and models used, rather than the conditions under which those "solutions" are applied. In both cases, people tend to believe factors that are more salient or visible play a bigger role in determining outcomes, compared to the less obvious enabling conditions such as a supportive organisational context (whatever the hell that means).

The lack of salience of enabling conditions means they *rarely get codified in procedures, governance models, bodies of knowledge or certifications.* Indeed, they do not because they cannot: they are very difficult to isolate and pin down. If this was not the case, Hackman, Kaplan and countless other researchers would have found the causal factors by now and we would have had empirical laws of management. Even when conditions are codified, they usually end up being platitudes such as "involve the right people" and "have a supportive organisational context".

We contend it is because of the difficulty of codifying enabling conditions that people tend to get drawn into low-value debates about whether method X is better than method Y, or whether the "5 pillars" to organisational nirvana is better than the "6 steps". Models and methods without due consideration of conditions will invariably fail to meet expectations and the cycle will start anew, with people latching onto the latest fad that bears an eerie similarity to one that came before.

The attribution error discussed above seems to stem from the deeply human need to understand and manipulate our environment. We're wired to seek causal explanations of what we observe because we yearn for certainty. This simple fact is what drives all management actions in the world of organisations. It is reinforced by our education because much of what we are taught in schools and universities is based on contrived situations in which cause and effect are obvious. Textbook problems are typically well-defined and have a correct (or at least, best) answer, leaving little room for ambiguity. Many people thus come out of management school believing the real world is that way too: that problems are given and that they always have well-defined answers. However, as Russell Ackoff (1986) put it (emphasis ours):

> "The major deficiencies in management education are not in what is taught but how it is taught. A major part of management education is devoted to trying to solve

problems given to students by teachers. As a result, students unconsciously come to believe that it is natural for problems to be given to them. *In the real world however, problems are seldom given; they must be taken. Nevertheless, students are neither taught nor learn how to take problems...*"

The inability to "take" a problem as Ackoff puts it, is a mindware gap, which means it is possible to learn how to do it. Indeed, the art of taking (or formulating) problems from raw experiences is what the art of *sensemaking* is all about. Sensemaking essentially consists of a collection of tools and techniques that can enable groups to arrive at a common understanding of complex phenomena, and hence, a shared commitment to an agreed solution. But this comes at a price: a key prerequisite for successful sensemaking is those who participate in the exercise must have a *healthy tolerance for ambiguity.*

Unfortunately, by the time many senior managers get to where they are, they are wedded to thinking in terms of clear-cut but simplistic causes and effects. Such thinking is understandable because it is an *extremely effective ambiguity coping mechanism.* Nonetheless, if the mindware gap of uncritical devotion to causal thinking is left unchecked, it tilts the cognitive seesaw towards a simplistic view of problem solving, which falls apart when applied to socially complex, highly nuanced situations which are the norm in large organisations. Those who cannot let go of this mode of thinking are invariably out of their depth in such situations because they are blind to the possibility that there might be multiple, equally valid, interpretations of what is going on. Interpretations that, if taken seriously, have a better chance of leading to more appropriate solutions.

In the next chapter we are going to focus on filling this mindware gap of understanding the nature of problems and why some are (much) harder to solve then others. In doing so, we aim to help readers learn how, as Ackoff put it, to "take" problems.

6

Wicked Problems

I'm a leader. Not a follower. Unless it's a dark place then screw it, you're going first.

—Bill Murray

No more ... please!

After reading the last chapter, your head might still be spinning from all the twists and turns we took as we examined various dilemmas in the natural and social sciences. Your brain may be hurting from having to assimilate new concepts while trying to understand the tangled issues that flow from them (if it's any consolation at all, our brains hurt too).

For some, it might be sobering and slightly depressing reading, while for others it might further confirm deeply held suspicions. Some might have agreed with us while others may have raised their defences and decided to drop a star or two from our Amazon book ratings in protest. If you are one of the latter, we'd like to remind you of what we learnt from neuroscience and cognitive science in Chapters 3 and 4 ... and urge you to make sure it's your System 2 brain determining our star ratings!

In any event, making some of our readers uncomfortable by triggering defensive instincts was precisely our intent! We wanted you to get a *feel* for these dilemmas as opposed to taking a "detached contemplation over involved action" style of thinking[27] that is so valued in scientific disciplines.

With that little preamble done, we want to put one of your mental seesaw kids through yet another fitness routine so to speak. We want you to think about a traumatic experience at work. We've all been there— that horrible queasy feeling where your heart is leaping out of your chest, where every fibre of your being wants to escape, but you know you can't. It could be that you have to break the news of a decision to people who will be deeply hurt by it or that you must confront a prickly issue that has long been an elephant in the room. It could even be something much more commonplace, like being required to work with others whose views and values are very different from yours. Situations like this can be so stressful that even thinking them invokes negative feelings. Whatever the issue is, we want you to keep it in mind as you read this chapter.

---

[27] In Chapter 3, we covered a paper by Chia and Holt who argued that university business schools privileged "detached contemplation" of theories, concepts and conceptual models over practical knowledge.

Now imagine you are sitting in a room with a bunch of people from different disciplines and professional backgrounds: psychologists, climate scientists, senior corporate executives, politicians and PR consultants (like the ones who served the tobacco industry). You have been tasked with improving the general public's perception of the facts about climate change. Clearly, those present will have strong and varied opinions on the main factors and causes of the issue. Some may feel that others in the room are part of the problem. Some may even feel this is a non-problem and still others may just want to get up and walk out of the room. To top it all, you are on a tight budget: which means if you do not come up with a strategy within a few meetings, funding is likely to be diverted elsewhere.

With that scene set, imagine one of the scientists saying "I think the first step for us all is to define the problem we are dealing with…"

How do you think the workshop would go?

Before you answer, review the various points we have made in the preceding chapters. Specifically, the points we ask you to keep in mind are:

- We all love our models and each discipline/thinking style not only has plenty to choose from, some models contradict others.

- Neurologically speaking, humans struggle to be task focused and empathy focused at the same time as they use different neural pathways that work against each other (think seesaws and kids).

- Also neurologically speaking, humans tend to struggle with ambiguity because it is processed in the primal parts of the brain that also regulate our emotions. Thus for many people, ambiguity creates a state of anxiety.

- Among our various coping mechanisms for ambiguity and anxiety are social defences such as avoidance behaviours, and the fetish-like use of models and process.

- Psychological needs influence our thinking dispositions and tolerance for ambiguity. For example: need for cognitive closure, need for approval and esteem, need for black/white facts, need for physics-like precision, and need for full understanding.

- High IQ does not automatically equate to good judgement and we are prone to many judgement-related biases.

- Our rationality (assuming we actually have some) is also influenced by cognitive miserliness, mindware gaps and contaminated mindware. Worse yet, what "contaminated" looks like is itself subjective.

- Many people have been educated in cause-effect thinking, influenced by models like Taylorism and Lean, seasoned with a generous sprinkling of physics envy. This results in a predisposition to strive for quantification where it may not be appropriate, completely overlooking the importance of context and conditions that are required for these models to work.

...and by the way, all that happens inside the head of just *one person*. In the scenario we just painted, a group of diverse people are grappling with the vexed problem of the standing of climate science in the broader community.

So with all these things in mind, we now ask you again. How do you think this workshop will go?

Welcome to the world of *wicked problems*. Such problems are characterised by a tangled mess of frustration, anxiety, mistrust and ambiguity-fuelled cognitive overload. This is a consequence of having many stakeholders with differing belief systems and conflicting world views, fuelled by assorted biases and mindware-gaps. To make matters worse, some of the latter are filled with dodgy mindware fillers—or to use a term we've used before—cognitive crap.

In such situations, it is difficult to get the group to agree on *what the problem is*. This, as you can imagine, makes it very difficult to work towards a solution because the solutions offered by each stakeholder will reflect how he or she views the problem. Thus a "solution" proposed by one person may well challenge beliefs that others hold to be inviolable truths.

To see how this comes about in concrete situations such as gun control, healthcare, drug trafficking, asylum seekers, or the conflicts like the one in Syria, consider our take on some of the commonly cited criteria for wicked problems:

- **A wicked problem can be described in numerous ways.** There is no comprehensive definition on what the problem is and the viewpoints that different people hold are often contradictory. Depending on which aspects of the problem one wants to emphasise, the approach taken to solving it will differ. Often people will articulate the problem in a way that suits their interests. In such situations it may well happen that what's an obvious fact to one person is extreme foolishness to another.

- **Each time a solution is proposed, the understanding of the problem changes.** There is no "stopping rule" in the sense that each new insight or solution reveals more aspects about the problem, leading to a situation in which people are loath to take action because additional analysis might increase the chances of finding a better solution. Analysis paralysis, anyone?

- **Solutions to wicked problems are never black and white.** Based on the above, proposed solutions to wicked problems are necessarily subjective. There is no objectively right answer that can be arrived at through a logical sequence of steps. Therefore, perceptions of a solution's effectiveness are likely to differ widely based on the personal interests, values, and ideology of the participants. Imagine what this does to someone who needs "objective" facts or has a strong need for cognitive closure.

- **Every solution to a wicked problem is a "one-shot operation"—you are never 100% sure and you cannot go back.** In a wicked problem, you can never reliably gauge cause and effect because there are many interdependent variables. Therefore, the result of any action is essentially unknowable; once you have taken action, the situation may change in unpredictable ways. Any solution, after being implemented, will generate waves of consequences that may yield undesirable repercussions which outweigh the expected advantages.

- **Wicked problems are essentially unique.** The ever-changing conditions afflicting wicked problems invariably challenge established world views or modes of thinking. They therefore require people to be open to new ideas and paradigms. Using "what worked elsewhere" or "what worked previously" will likely not work because each circumstance is unique. A related point—and one that is relevant to those who are wedded to solely using a scientific approach to problem solving—is that this makes solutions to such problems hard to falsify and or replicate.

- **Every wicked problem can be considered to be a symptom of another problem.** This refers to the fact that a wicked problem can usually be traced back to a deeper underlying problem that itself consists of many more interlocking sub-problems. Eventually the problem becomes so complex is it beyond the cognitive capacity of any one person to understand.

- **With wicked problems, you are penalised for being wrong.** The scientific method permits people to be wrong—indeed, that's the point of falsifiability and replicability. With a wicked problem, being wrong is personally costly as problem solvers are invariably held responsible for the unanticipated consequences of their solutions. This tends to amplify the ambiguity quotient and reinforce analysis-paralysis—people are reluctant to act because they will be held responsible (or worse, blamed) for their actions.

It is really important to note that "wicked" is not the only term used to describe these sorts of problems. In our last book (Culmsee & Awati, 2013), we noted that a number of researchers from diverse disciplines independently recognised that problems or situations could be classified along a spectrum of difficulty like we just described. Figure 6.1 lists each end of the spectrum of problems, along with whoever coined the term. All are essentially talking about the same thing.

Researchers	Left Extreme	Right Extreme
Rittel/Webber	Tame problem	Wicked problem
Simon	Programmed decision	Non Programmed decision
Ackoff	Problem	Mess
Ravetz	Technical Problem	Practical Problem
Heifetz	Technical Problem	Adaptive Problem
Checkland	Hard Systems	Soft Systems
Johnson	Problems to solve	Polarities to manage
Von Foerster	Decidable questions	Undecidable questions
Bohr, Bak or Snowden (take your pick)	Complicated	Complex

Figure 6.1: Problem category names and the people who coined them.

The categorisations in Figure 6.1 are all essentially making a distinction between problems or situations which can be approached in a *consistently replicable way* (just like physics for the most part!) and those that cannot. With the problems described in the middle column, one can in effect, "crank the handle to produce the sausage"—they are problems where time-tested techniques work just fine and are rarely controversial. These problems are also the domain of *best practices*. That said, these problems are not automatically easy. Indeed, they can be extremely challenging and require specialist skills and a good deal of foresight and insight (just like physics for the most part!). It is critically important to remember that just because a problem is tame or technical, it does not mean it is easy; there is a good reason why people often use the expression "Well I am no rocket scientist..."

It is also important to note that the table is not so much about two distinct types of problems, *but two ends of a spectrum of problem types*. In other words, there are varying degrees of "wickedness". In fact, some problems, both organisationally and at societal level, can cause an extreme polarisation of opinion that they go beyond being merely wicked, they become *toxic*. If wicked problems were ten on a one-to-ten scale, toxic problems would rate eleven. Figure 6.2 illustrates the idea of a spectrum of problems between tame, wicked and toxic. We hereby dub it the "Culmsee and Awati 'It Goes to Eleven' Model of Problem Ambiguity"[28].

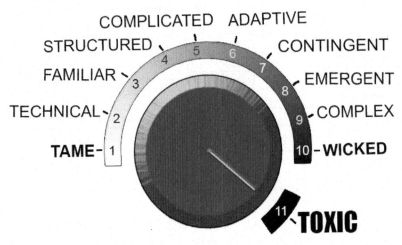

Figure 6.2: The Culmsee and Awati "It Goes to Eleven" Model of Problem Ambiguity

The disabling power of wickedness

In the last chapter, we introduced you to Richard Hackman (2012), whose seminal work on high performing teams tells us to focus on creating conditions that foster high-quality collaborative work, rather than look for those chimerical causal levers that magically turn on a collaborative mindset. Consider now, a situation involving elements of

---

[28] In the 1984 mockumentary/rockumentary "This Is Spinal Tap", one of the band members pointed out that his guitar amplifier was so cool that it had the highest volume setting of eleven, unlike run-of-the-mill amplifiers with a maximum volume of ten. When asked if the label on the volume knob makes any difference to actual volume, the band member looked puzzled and repeated "These go to eleven."

wickedness. In this circumstance, enabling conditions might not only be absent or suppressed, but some of them might become *disabling conditions*.

The most likely-to-be-affected condition is that of a "compelling purpose". Hackman spoke of the need for a purpose that "is clear, challenging, and consequential", one which energises team members and engages them. But a wicked problem by its very nature works against this condition because the problem cannot be pinned down. It is very hard to have a compelling purpose when the very nature of the problem varies depending on who you ask and how you ask it.

We contend that without the purpose condition being met, it is impossible for any of Hackman's other conditions to be fulfilled. For example, Hackman characterised "real team" as interdependence among members, clear membership boundaries and membership stability over time. Interdependence simply means that members are mutually reliant on each-other, which is hard to do when the problem is slippery, facts are disputed and mistrust about others' intentions abound.

In his "right people" condition, Hackman spoke of task expertise, self-organisation and skill in working collaboratively. But when there is ambiguity-driven anxiety, amplified by the wicked problem characteristic of not having the "right to be wrong", and combined with the adaptive and evolving nature of wicked problems, the skills required are usually not understood or appreciated upfront. Even the popular teamwork virtue of being self-organised is undermined in a wicked context. Self-organised teams can self-organize only around a common compelling purpose. When that is missing, individuals will inevitably take self-interest driven unilateral actions that erode trust—the bedrock of self-organizing teams. Self-interest will invariably trump self-organisation in wicked situations.

On intention and wickedness in organisations

In view of all the above, it's no surprise that wicked problems are not "solved" in the traditional sense of the word. In fact, even characterising wickedness as a "problem" makes contentious assumptions, since some stakeholders may believe that there is no problem at all (the stance of certain politicians on climate change is a good example of this). As a result, a wicked problem or "mess" can only be *managed*. It cannot be comprehensively solved since taking action a) assumes that there is agreement on what the problem is and b) will have unforeseen "waves of consequences".

Because wicked problems are managed rather than solved, much of the literature on the topic focuses on the importance of facilitating shared understanding, leveraging group wisdom, end-to-end stakeholder involvement in the solution and collective sensemaking to help people come to grips with what they are dealing with. Virtually all the techniques are based on open dialogue. But the inconvenient truth is that open dialogue is much easier to talk about than to actually achieve. In wicked situations, the widely varying stakeholder intentions that drive defensive behaviours usually come in the way of open dialogue. Often, stakeholder groups with strong vested interest will manipulate conditions so as to achieve their aims. The tobacco industry provides a great example of this because their *intent* was to raise significant public doubt about the dangers of their product. They were able to do this by exploiting inherent weaknesses of the scientific method and human susceptibility to ambiguity. Although they clothed their arguments in scientific terms, there was *no intention* on their part to determine a definitive link between their product and health issues. In fact, their intent was just the opposite: to prolong doubt as long as possible.

Interestingly, just as the scientific method can be leveraged against itself, the tobacco industry also showed us how softer, more collaborative approaches can be manipulated too. It is possible to run collaborative workshops for years without getting anywhere. Had they chosen to, tobacco industry decision-makers could have run collaborative workshops in such a way that the causal link between tobacco and health concerns remained ambiguous.

The reality is that in such situations it's *doubtful that any collaborative approach founded on dialogue would work*. Unfortunately, without a mind reading device, a Wikileaks expose or convenient industrial espionage, intention cannot be trumped by inviting people to change their minds and expecting them to be rational about doing so. As we all know, it is all too easy to nod assent while plotting dissent. Recall the lesson from our alien fearing, tin-foil hat wearing friend in Chapter 4. From their perspective, they are being instrumentally rational if their actions help them fulfil their intentions (and the hell with everyone else).

This appears to lead us to a disappointing conclusion. Some wicked problems, and all toxic problems, are essentially no-win situations—even when using all those wonderful collaborative approaches suggested by the literature.

Yet all hope is not lost...

You cannot trump intent, but...

Some readers might consider our treatment of strategies for dealing with wicked problems as a bit harsh ... and it is. So let's now see how one can save the situation. In relation to our discussion this far, there are three really important facts readers need to remember.

Firstly, in many scenarios—in particular, the organisational scenarios that are our main concern in this book—most people genuinely want to see better outcomes. In other words, *there is genuine intent to find a meaningful way forward.* While the problem might be complex and challenging, and people might have fundamental disagreements, resentments and trust issues vis-à-vis other participants, these *can often be overcome when there is genuine intent to do so.* This was established by Elinor Ostrom who was awarded the 2009 Nobel Prize for Economics for her research demonstrating that different stakeholders can converge around a common purpose even if they had very different motives for doing so, provided that the conditions of *trust* and *reciprocity*[29] can be established. In such cases, collaborative sensemaking approaches, along with well-designed governance structures to foster these conditions—like those described in our first book—are extremely valuable and can lead to real breakthroughs.

---

[29] Reciprocity refers to the adage of doing unto others as you would have them do unto you. It essentially refers to the point we made a few lines earlier about making it difficult for a party to act unilaterally without undermining their own positions.

Secondly, in organisational settings, problems are usually not as wicked as they appear to be. Most organisational problems rate much lower than eleven on our patented problem wickedness scale. In such situations, mindware gaps can be filled, cognitive crap flushed out, anxiety can be managed and fetish objects can be let go if needed ... with a bit of coaxing. We'll say more about this in the next chapter.

Finally, even if the problem is toxic (rated level 11), there are things one can do to reduce toxicity or at least, the perception of toxicity. While intent cannot be trumped, one can take a cue from Hackman and *foster conditions that shift intent*. You don't change people's minds by telling them to change their minds. Instead, you create the conditions that enable them to change their minds of their own free will. The story of our friendly neighbourhood manager Edwin in Chapter 2 is a simple example. Once he was given a KPI that measured employee retention, his behaviour changed overnight from his previous approaches. In organisation land, there is a lot of truth to Goldratt's memorable one-liner, "Tell me how you measure me and I'll tell you how I behave" (Goldratt, 1990).

For a better example of how conditions shift intent in the context of a global wicked problem, consider the issue of public perception of climate change we mentioned earlier in this chapter. It has been proven via a combination of freedom of information requests, leaks and legal records that some fossil fuel industry players used the same tactics as the tobacco lobby in exploiting physics envy and doubt, even using the same consultants who helped the Tobacco industry!

However, while they are very powerful and wield huge influence, these companies *do not control the entire playing field*. One particular area that they could not directly control were the innovations, disruptions and economies of scale that were occurring in the renewables sector. In recent years, the *idea* of supporting renewables has won the hearts and minds of *enough people* to cause a virtuous cycle that grows the industry, thereby driving down costs, fostering innovations and influencing public policy, all of which leads to further growth. As a result, renewables now not only have an appealing narrative, but are also becoming more affordable.

As we discovered in the last chapter, surveys continue to indicate scepticism in the general population about the validity of claims of human-caused global warming. Nevertheless, many people actually like the idea of generating their own energy, and on a more practical note, saving money. Entrepreneurs, investors and financiers react to increased confidence with their wallets. This further drives confidence and growth in renewables while increasing critical scrutiny of the fossil fuels sector. For example: over the years this book was written, various fund managers around the world have publicly stated they are divesting fossil fuels investments from their portfolios[30]. This in turn, creates issues for these companies because they are seen as riskier investment propositions, which reduces their credit ratings, increases their cost of capital and making it more difficult for them to do business.

Under these conditions, many fossil fuel companies have abandoned the "delay and deny" approach because it no longer served their interests the way it once did. Many have moved to an "embrace and extend" approach, like BP, which rebranded itself with a sunflower logo and the slogan "Beyond Petroleum". In fact, in a 2002 speech at Stanford University, BP's then chief executive, Lord John Browne stated:

"Companies composed of highly skilled and trained people can't live in denial of mounting evidence gathered by hundreds of the most reputable scientists in the world" (Frey D. , 2002).

Many other oil companies have made similar statements, which interestingly and somewhat paradoxically, seems to indicate more consensus on climate change among fossil fuel industry players than the general population. While this does not mean for a moment that these organisations are suddenly going to go totally green and abandon their old business models, it demonstrates that when conditions change, previously unnegotiable positions can turn negotiable.

---

[30] https://en.wikipedia.org/wiki/Fossil_fuel_divestment

The ethics of shaping intentions

This brings us to the crux of this book. While the preceding chapters have offered you some (sometimes not-so-serious) models and ideas that can help you in understanding behaviours and norms that occur in your project, workplace or community, the next chapter will demonstrate their utility in the art of *manipulating those conditions.*

Everything we have covered so far, including seesaw kids, ambiguity intolerance, fetish objects, and the limits of rationality, give us *tons* of juicy ammo. Not only can we mess with left-brain rationalists, we can just as easily mess with the right brained humanists too.

Now some readers might feel uncomfortable with our use of the word "manipulating" in the context of conditions. To be sure, we could have used less forceful words like "shaping", "influencing" and "facilitating" conditions, and we could have framed this book in a more positive light such as "how to get the best out of your team", but doing so obscures a key point.

It is patently obvious that the subtle art of management—which in our view, always involves the manipulation of conditions—can be used to serve different intentions. In other words, any advice we offer can absolutely be used just as much for evil as for good. How you apply a manipulative technique, is entirely an ethical question which you have to figure out for yourself. One way to look through the lens of "manipulation" is to heed the advice of famed polymath Hans von Foerster (2003), who observed that *how* a decision is made and implemented says more about the decision-maker than the soundness of the decision itself.

On the other hand, you could also take a different view and simply ask: why should all the narcissists, psychopaths and political spin-doctors have all the fun? It is high time more ethically intentioned folks get a chance too.

7

Good Teddies, Bad Teddies

"The greater the ambiguity, the greater the pleasure."

—Milan Kundera

May the force be with you...

As practitioners, we have applied various popular and not-so-popular facilitation, management, and problem solving techniques in diverse situations. In the process, we have learnt how to get the best out of them through trial and (frequent) error. On reflection, most of the errors we made were, in one way or another, related to *inadvertently undermining the conditions needed for the approaches to work*. In view of our discussion of wicked problems in the last chapter, it should be no surprise that any tool, model, or method can be rendered ineffective, or even backfire, if the conditions to support it are absent.

In this chapter, we are going to examine how *ambiguity can be harnessed to influence a situation*. As we discovered in Chapter 3, ambiguity is a powerful, primal force that has a significant effect on, and even drives, human behaviour. Understandably, ambiguity is generally seen as something negative, something to be avoided. However, as we hope to show you in this chapter, it is a force that can be also used in positive ways. Ambiguity can paralyse action, but when appropriately harnessed, can catalyse it too.

So how can we master this mysterious force of ambiguity, as a Jedi Master would channel The Force? One thing's for certain, you won't be using light sabres (sorry Star Wars fans). Believe it or not, the weapons of choice for Ambiguity Jedis are teddy bears!

Figure 7.1: The preferred tool of the Ambiguity Jedi

Teddy bears?

In Chapter 3, we mentioned Wastell and his notion of *methodology as fetish*, where he makes an analogy between objects that help kids develop self-reliance (such as teddy bears or security blankets) and the processes and methodologies that people use in the corporate world. He argued that models, methodologies, processes, or even consultants serve as psychological support for denizens of corporate-land, much in the same way as teddy bears or security blankets provide three year-olds with a sense of security that serves to facilitate emotional development.

It is common to see such corporate teddy bears in group settings through the positive reactions you get when you honour them and the negative reactions when you don't. If you have ever been cut off mid-conversation, taken to task for using a term in the wrong context, told that your suggestion "isn't the way we do things here," or challenged on a question you posed, chances are you inadvertently stepped on someone's teddy bear.

To reiterate, a corporate teddy bear is a process, methodology or behaviour that is followed, not because it leads to better outcomes, but *because it helps its adherents cope with ambiguity*. The art of harnessing ambiguity in constructive ways—i.e. ways that create conditions conducive to tackling complex issues—lies in the following actions, each of which we will examine in detail in this chapter:

1. Handing out Teddy Bears
2. Taking away Teddy Bears
3. Swapping Teddy Bears

We believe the pinnacle of corporate Jedi mindcraft lies in knowing which of the three actions—hand out, take away or swap—is effective in specific situations. Our aim in this chapter is to give you an introduction to this secret Jedi knowledge[31] which will enable you to help groups

---

[31] Like Jedi knowledge, the art of reframing ambiguity cannot be taught, but can be learnt. The vignettes that follow describe practical situations involving

harness ambiguity by *reframing* situations. Let's see what this looks like by going through the three major ways in which you can use teddy bears in organisation-land…

Handing out Teddy Bears

Our own experiences suggest that one of the best things you can do to reduce ambiguity in a group is to *find the teddy bear your audience likes and symbolically hand it to them upfront.*

Teddy bears can take many diverse forms. As we mentioned in Chapter 3, they can be the expression of an idea, a process, a book, the organisation chart, a methodology or even a person. All it may take to symbolically hand a teddy to a receptive participant or audience is the right slide in a deck, a reference to a methodology they are familiar with, a sound-bite from a management guru, or even the use of certain terms (such as "process improvement") in the right context.

As an example, consider a facilitated strategic planning session in an organisation that is traditional, hierarchical, and highly process driven. Regardless of how the facilitator intends to conduct the session, it helps to begin by showing a standard sequential management model that is familiar to the group, such as the one shown in Figure 7.2.

The key point is the facilitator *spends very little time in explaining the model as it is already familiar to participants.* The intention here is to symbolically hand the group a teddy bear—an orienting object that is familiar and comfortable before moving on to new territory. Whether the facilitator believes in the model or not is not the point; the purpose is not to educate, but to *reduce anxiety* within the group. It is not so much about what the model conveys, but simply *that it is there* … indeed, one can almost picture a group of workshop participants clutching their old-new teddies to their chest.

---

the reframing of ambiguous situations. Our intent is to help you recognize and influence such situations in your work and even your personal life.

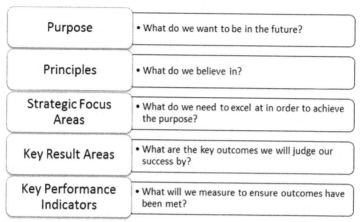

Figure 7.2: A standard strategy model linking vision to KPIs

Once the teddy has been handed out, it becomes easier for the facilitator to segue into other techniques and activities, even those that may be unfamiliar or uncomfortable for the group. This is because the teddy bear serves to reassure participants that whatever happens next is both legitimate and will remain within familiar boundaries, even though it may well be unfamiliar. As an example, consider this excerpt from a facilitation session:

> Facilitator: "Now we all know that the business-as-usual approach is to start at the top by talking about vision and purpose, and then move logically downward into principles, focus areas and KPIs. However, today I'd like to invite you all to consider an approach that I find has worked well for other organisations facing complex challenges similar to yours. We will initially spend some time around the focus areas, and see what this tells us about vision, principles and KPIs as the discussion unfolds…"

If you read carefully, there is more than one teddy being handed out here. In addition to the model of Figure 7.2 which is a *legitimisation teddy*, "business-as-usual" is being framed in a mildly pejorative way. This teddy—which we will call a *"hipster teddy"* for its non-conformist leanings—is designed for corporate agitators who are pushing for a change in the status quo and like to challenge the "same old thinking". You might think this is too subtle, but one of the advantages of confirmation bias (one of the biases we examined in Chapter 4) is that people tend to hear what supports their pre-existing views. Thus with some luck, the corporate agitator will regard you as a potential co-revolutionary. Yet at the same time, by likening the approach to one being successfully used elsewhere, one subtly addresses the FOMO (Fear of Missing Out) attitude of others who may be more conservative.

Finally, the use of invitational language reminds people that they are being asked to exercise a free choice. This is important because, as we discovered in our exploration of psychological needs in Chapter 4, people like to feel in control of their choices and actions.

Once you are familiar with the notion of teddy bears, you will see them popping up everywhere in your workplace and beyond. Indeed, they are likely to show up in any situation that involves even a hint of ambiguity. Many of the topics we have explored in this book, such as seesaw kids, organisational defence routines, psychological needs, physics envy, falsifiability and wicked problems, *are designed to help you recognise the teddy bears that might work in specific situations.* Once you have made an assessment of a suitable teddy, you can figure out ways to hand them out. This could happen in a workshop scenario, meeting, or even a one-on-one conversation.

Remember though, teddy bears handed out this way are essentially distractions—ways to focus attention and reduce anxiety levels, at least initially. Just as a child can be distracted by a toy or nursery rhyme to make taking medicine easier, so too can adults when they are being administered a dose of organisational medicine.

Teddy handout worst practices...

Now that you've seen the simplicity of handing out teddy bears, you're probably thinking that there's nothing particularly profound about it. You may have also recognised situations in which you have handed out some yourself. We agree, but we also contend that the art of handing out teddy bears is a subtle one that is better understood by looking at common ways practitioners get it wrong—i.e. when they end up amplifying ambiguity and destroying the conditions required for getting a desired outcome. Our intent in illustrating these worst practices is to show you what *not* to do when handing out teddies.

One of the most common and gravest teddy handout sins is to peddle platitudes. This often takes the form of a speech (with an accompanying PowerPoint deck) given by a leader when an organisation is undertaking a large change initiative, such as a restructure. While the intention is to provide reassurance, the use of clichés like "Our people are our greatest asset", "This is a career opportunity…" and "Every journey starts with a single step…" end up having precisely the opposite effect on the rank and file employees who are most directly affected by the change. The platitudes peddled here are not real teddies because the only person they reassure is the one handing them out.

Another very common pitfall that practitioners who've learnt a new tool, method or supermodel tend to fall into, is believing everybody else will love their technique as much as they do. Such folks tend to inflict their newly learnt wisdom on others with great passion, using verbose language peppered with new and often unduly long words. Despite their genuine intent to help others make sense of a complex situation, they end up being less than successful because no one quite understands what they are on about and wish they would just shut up.

One reason this happens is that many problem solving techniques are rooted in academic disciplines that use esoteric concepts and terminology, such as *complexity theory, operations research* or *cybernetics*. While the concepts and methods are often useful, one needs to invest the time to understand and assimilate them—and the learning curve can be quite steep.

Confounding this problem is the "curse of knowledge", a cognitive bias we first mentioned in Chapter 4. This is where our enthusiastic evangelists, so enamoured with their newfound teddies, find it extremely difficult to think about problems from the perspective of others who may not be as "enlightened". Concepts that are blindingly obvious to evangelists often seem bewilderingly complex to others. What better way to undermine conditions than to hit people with a heavy conceptual brick while they are already trying to come to grips with ambiguity and the political dynamics of a wicked situation. It is easy to see how, despite best intentions, this might have an adverse effect on the conditions for dealing with complex organisational issues.

Another trap to watch out for is the method evangelist—the guy who ends up advocating his favourite teddy as a panacea: the one teddy to rule them all. Much like those hammer-wielders who perceive all problems to be nails, such folks tend to default to their preferred method (*their* teddy bears) without thinking about its appropriateness for the situation at hand.

Besides overlooking context, another problem with panacea teddies is that using a particular method or technique too often runs a very real risk of diminishing returns. This is essentially a problem of overexposure. The first time a group is exposed to a new technique or approach there can be a high degree of interest because of the novelty of the experience. Unfortunately, with new teddies, the initial sense of freshness tends to decrease as the technique is used repeatedly. In fact, there seems to be a law of problem solving in socially complex situations that *using the same techniques with the same groups will render them less effective as time goes on.* Initial enthusiasm will rapidly be replaced with a feeling of disengagement or *alienated compliance*—which is our term for the (dare we say) common attitude in organisations wherein people follow a process because they have to. Pushed to its logical end, people will end up loathing the teddy.

This highlights one of the most important principles that practitioners and methodology freaks tend to overlook. Management models and problem solving approaches are often subject to increasing entropy, in that *they all tend to dissipate the constructive energy they initially harness.* In other words, much like a good bottle of single malt scotch, one can have too much of a good thing. Indeed, our experience with a wide variety of management techniques suggests this is so common, it should be enshrined as a *fundamental law of management* (along with the even more fundamental law that any declared management law is always wrong!)

Given this, the best one can do is to choose the theory (or technique) *that best fits the situation.* While you may strongly identify with a particular model or method, it is important to realise there are many others that could yield similar (or even better) results … yes, even if the concepts and terminology they use don't appeal to you. The implication of this "law" of management is that you have to put in a lot of hard work to read and practice many different approaches, thus building up your "method arsenal". The priceless benefit of this, however, is the broadening of one's perspective on the different kinds of wicked problems one is likely to face in organisation-land and the different approaches available to tackle them. Most important, it gives the practitioner a tacit understanding of which ones would work best for a given situation and audience. In terms of our teddy bear metaphor, practitioners need to carry around a bunch of teddies and know where they might work well and where they might not.

We've covered quite a bit of territory here, so let's do a recap of what we have learnt so far about handing out teddies…

1. Don't hit people with conceptual bricks (unless they enjoy it … for example, if you're dealing with a bunch of academics, the conceptual brick is the teddy).
2. You will always love your own teddy more than everybody else will (and if you have a child in the house you already know that!).
3. Learn to appreciate others' teddies, even if they are not as cute as yours.
4. Don't be a one-teddy child as the teddy is not for you anyway. Keep a few handy, you will need them. Using the same teddy over and over again will dissipate the energy and enthusiasm that it initially harnesses.
5. Choose teddies based not on your preferences, but on the problem at hand and the disposition of your audience.
6. Above all, do not be a platitude peddler!

Teddy handout examples

Given our learnings so far, let's look at another teddy bear example. This is one we have found to be of great utility when public sector agencies are about to undertake a complex initiative. See if you can guess why...

Figure 7.3: A highly useful teddy bear from the Australian Public Sector

Figure 7.3 is the cover of a freely available discussion paper written by the Australian Public Service Commission (2007) on understanding wicked problems and how to tackle them. It emphasises the importance of collaborative strategies, holistic thinking and working across-organisational boundaries. The great thing about this paper, from a teddy bear handout perspective, is its utility for a wide variety of people. For the conceptual types, the vast, rich literature on wicked problems helps meet their cognition and legitimation needs ("finally a rigorous explanation that makes sense!"), while the action heroes[32] have a ready-made, neatly packaged solution written by authors with the right pedigree ("The policy wonks wrote it—that's good enough for me!").

Paul often uses this document in workshops in a similar manner to the strategic plan of Figure 7.2. By handing out this teddy bear at the start, the workshop is now framed in a way that reduces up-front ambiguity for many participants and legitimises what comes next. Indeed, appreciating the situation and framing a response appropriately is the key to harnessing ambiguity.

In another example, this time in the private sector, Kailash used various teddies to frame a problem and its solution. He was involved in developing a global service centre in Asia for a multinational organisation. The initial mandate was to keep it "unofficial" (which meant there was no budget allocated) and do it in a way that did not "rock the organisational status quo" too much. The reason was driven by a fear that folks in head office might feel unsettled were they to become aware of the initiative, primarily because they might view it as moving their jobs to low cost countries.

To address this, Kailash handed out several teddy bears, starting with a classic—the *"Calm down, it's just a pilot"* teddy. That is, he framed the initiative as a pilot project to *test* innovative new ways of collaborative outsourcing. This teddy worked a treat because a) managers in corporate liked the "innovative" implications; b) they liked the obvious cost advantage (which was stated, but in a low-key way); and c) employees in corporate did not feel that their jobs were on the line.

The pilot teddy bear was critical because without it, the initiative would have been opposed or undermined from the start. But the pilot merely got the centre approved. With no budget, Kailash had to get people who had money to buy in to the idea of getting work done via the nascent service centre ... more teddies were needed.

Firstly, Kailash developed marketing material including brochures and even a short video extolling the qualities of the location, including cost. Knowing that cost control was high on every manager's performance objectives, he framed it as helping meet their KPI. This *"It*

---

[32] Action heroes, as their name suggests, are people who tend to jump into solving a problem, often without spending adequate time in analyzing and understanding. All organisations have a fair number of these people around, you'll usually find them lurking in the ranks of front line and mid-level management.

helps you meet your KPI" teddy bear directly addressed their performance objectives while avoiding the inference it was all about cost control. In essence, Kailash was able to use the obvious elephant in the room to his advantage. i.e. "It's not about cost" (but it really is).

Secondly, Kailash used another teddy that works very well for people who are driven by the psychological need for approval and esteem. He used the *"This could be your crowning achievement"* teddy bear. This essentially entails selling a future state where the initiative, after its implementation, is seen as an awesome achievement, with recognition and general praise for those courageous pioneers who made it possible. To do this, Kailash socialised the idea of setting up a centre of excellence for a particular business need within the service centre. This teddy bear speaks to an aspirational goal that goes beyond KPIs. It appeals to managers who see themselves as rising stars in the company, and would like to do things that would make *their* managers sit up and take notice.

The final teddy bear Kailash used, we like to call the *"Nobel Prize"* teddy bear. This powerful teddy provides a *sense of authority and legitimacy*. Kailash used Transaction Cost Theory (Williamson, 2010) as a basis for building his business case. The fact that the theory was proposed by a Nobel Laureate gave the business case a legitimacy that went beyond the tired old arguments trotted out by Big 4 consultancies. Of course, his stakeholders were not particularly interested in the theory itself, but were suitably impressed with its Nobel Prize-winning pedigree—after all, if no-one gets fired for hiring IBM, who's going to argue with a dude who won a Nobel Prize?

The critical aspect about this teddy is that it *feels authoritative and rational*. Kailash used it to provide the narrative of rationality to those who were less convinced by the pilot and crowning achievement teddies. In fact, Paul uses the pedigree behind the Wicked Problem paper mentioned in Figure 7.3 in a very similar way. The point, in both these situations (and most others), is to reframe it in a way that makes people see things in a different light.

The "Pilot", "Crowning Achievement", "KPI" and "Nobel prize" teddies worked their magic and Kailash was able to get the centre off the ground and running within a year. As it turned out, a couple of years later, folks in corporate were happy to work with people in the service centre because by then, they realised that the service centre *extended* their capabilities rather than *replaced* them.

Meet some of the teddy family...

Now that we have seen some real-world examples of handing out teddies, let's recap some of them. No doubt there are many more teddies out there, but the ones listed in Figure 7.4 are common ones we have encountered in our work...

Figure 7.4: A sample of common handout teddies

Figure 7.4 also lists psychological needs or drivers addressed by each teddy. Indeed, the crux of managing ambiguity is to understand the underlying fears it generates, and then figure out which teddy bears will serve to reframe the situation in a way that allays those fears. Since a group consists of diverse people with different personalities, you will invariably find that you have to deploy a range of teddy bears, each one addressing a specific sub-group's need.

Taking Away Teddy Bears

Now that we have learnt about how teddy bears can be handed out, let's examine how we can harness the power of ambiguity by *taking them away*. In practice, this entails disrupting the sort of defence mechanisms we first encountered in the teaching hospital example from Chapter 3. In that case, the hospital was plagued with institutionalised defences that unintentionally subverted the primary objective of good patient outcomes. Ironically, the defence mechanisms actually increased staff anxiety instead of reducing it, as evidenced by a systemic problem of low morale and high staff turnover. As a reminder, the defensive practices were:

- Breaking up work into smaller, excruciatingly detailed tasks and procedures that were ritualistically followed (the *"Just give me a work instruction"* teddy).
- Excessive checks, counter-checks and purposeful obscurity of roles and responsibilities to avoid the weight and accountability of decision making (the *"Safety in numbers"* teddy).
- Reverse delegation, where trivial decisions were pushed up the management hierarchy so as to disclaim responsibility for outcomes (the *"I need to check this with my supervisor"* teddy).

Although seventy years have passed since this famous case study, similar defensive teddies are being held dear by many people in organisations of today. If anything, defensive routines have become more sophisticated and subtle. Consider these examples:

- Pulling the "Don't bring us a problem unless you have a solution" line (the *"Put up or shut up"* teddy).

- Disclaiming responsibility for making a decision, via "I don't make the rules" or "I am just following orders" (the *"Soldier"* teddy).

- Pinning the issue on an outside party or individual, thereby disowning responsibility (the *"Scapegoat"* teddy).

- Using standards and process as a means to close down lines of enquiry or to take options off the table, via the "You can't do that, because of the standard" (the *"Standard says no"* teddy).

- Focusing only on the factual, technical parts of the problem and wilfully ignoring the adaptive or complex parts (the *"Just give me the facts"* teddy).

Figure 7.5 presents a gallery of common teddy bears that have a tendency to go rogue—i.e. have an effect opposite to the one intended. However, it is important to point out that no teddy is inherently good or bad, it is the context that determines goodness or lack thereof. For example, one might deploy the Hipster Teddy seen in Figure 7.4 by making a proposed approach sound cool and contemporary. On the other hand, a Hipster Teddy fan who is pushing for a cool new idea to be implemented just because it is cool rather than benefits afforded by it, needs to have the teddy taken away double quick. Similarly, a common rogue teddy scenario involving the KPI and FOMO teddies is when an organisation measures anything and everything, not because they are the right things to measure, but simply because they are easy to measure … and if you don't do Big Data Analytics, you *are* going to be left behind.

Type of Teddy		
Work Instruction Teddy	Safety in Numbers Teddy	Scapegoat Teddy

Need Satisfied		
Need for cognitive closure	Need for security/being part of the crowd	Restore order Deflect focus

Type of Teddy		
Put up or shut up Teddy	Power Teddy	Solider Teddy

Need Satisfied		
Need for clarity	Need for control/esteem	Need to deflect responsibility

Figure 7.5: The rogue teddy gallery

A common theme among these rogue teddies, is that they serve to maintain a sense of control by *diverting and deflecting attention from ambiguity*. They "situate people's appreciation" instead of getting them to appreciate the situation. To do the latter, people must confront ambiguity, which means they have to let go of their teddies. How do we get them to do that?

One thing is for sure: never disparage the teddy itself. All that will do is make people clutch it all the more tightly. Instead, we now offer you several subtle teddy removal approaches that have a much better chance of succeeding.

Shift the focus from the teddy bear

Anybody who has ever questioned a fetishised process or methodology has likely encountered the classic "you don't understand it at all" defence mechanism from its proponents. This is a very common response from people clutching the "Just give me a work instruction", "Standard says no", "Thou must do it this way" or "Thou must follow this process exactly" teddies.

Unfortunately, this defence commonly ends in long and pointless arguments on minutiae that are oxygen to process freaks. So instead of calling out a problematic aspect of a process or methodology, a better way to disarm such teddies is to ask the following question:

> "What is the *intent* of this [strategy, process, standard, or method]?"

This question is framed in a way that draws attention away from the teddy bear itself and focuses on what's actually important: the *difference in outcome* that the process or standard is intended to achieve. Inevitably, answers will start with verbs like "improving", "reducing", "increasing" or "eliminating". Aside from being measurable—provided the answer is not a platitude[33] like "improved efficiency"—this opens two lines of enquiry. You can ask whether:

1. The stated intent is currently being met (and explore why it is, or is not) or
2. You can suggest "Well, what if I can demonstrate how we can meet that intent?" using an alternative. This invites the teddy

---

[33] See Chapter 2 of (Culmsee and Awati 2013) for much more on disarming platitudes

owner to consider your proposal in terms of the yardstick *they* have set.

We call this question the "FUD[34] buster" and it is one of a number of *powerful questions* that we find very useful in ambiguity management. We will soon cover other powerful questions, including one that is very effective in dealing with platitudinous answers. For now, it should be noted that if people have trouble answering the FUD buster question, it is a likely sign that the standard or process they are citing is being used as a teddy bear: that is, it is being used for anxiety reduction rather than achieving concrete, useful outcomes.

Stress test via scenarios

Another approach which is more time consuming but avoids the "but you don't understand" comeback, is to paint a scenario and ask the teddy fan how it should be handled. The idea here is to present the person with a scenario they have not fully considered before. Typically, most process/model/standard fans believe their teddy can handle every conceivable scenario, but have not rigorously tested this belief. Like the FUD buster question, this strategy calls bullshit on the teddy without actually disparaging it.

To illustrate, some time back Paul worked with an organisation that had implemented the ITIL framework.[35] The process owner was implementing it for the first time and happened to have imbibed gallons of ITIL Kool-Aid. Unsurprisingly, his grand vision for implementation was going to result in significant work for many people across the department, both in terms of creating and maintaining documentation as well as the day-to-day overhead of adhering to the elaborate process. Paul saw various issues with this approach, but committed the cardinal sin of querying a problematic part of the process, highlighting what he thought was a gap. Very quickly the proponent became agitated and threw the "You don't understand it" defence back at him.

---

[34] FUD: Fear, Uncertainty and Doubt: https://goo.gl/xNhX4x
[35] https://en.wikipedia.org/wiki/ITIL

Realising just how tightly the ITIL teddy was being held, Paul apologised, waited a couple of days and then invited the proponent to help him work through a real-world scenario. Well aware the scenario was going to cause problems for our ITIL hero, Paul took the approach of being an ITIL novice, seeking advice on how the standard should be applied to this specific situation. Fairly quickly, our hero realised his idealised model had a gap, and suggested changes that addressed the very issues Paul tried had to call out originally.

The enemy of my enemy is...

Another teddy removal approach that is useful for situations in which scapegoat teddies abound (e.g. "It's all IT's fault"), is to *shift focus to an external threat*—a clear and present danger that cannot be controlled by anyone.

The power of a common threat or sense of urgency to bring feuding parties together cannot be overstated. As an example, one of Paul's clients hired a new CEO who engaged outside consultants to conduct a comprehensive organisation-wide review and restructure. The process was brutal for the first division that went through it, as it was disbanded and absorbed into other areas of the organisation. The head of another division that Paul worked with decided, together with his direct reports, to institute their own review. The rationale was simple: better to be proactive and address issues on their own terms rather than suffer the fate of the first division. Despite the division having some tricky inter-departmental issues of its own, the external threat of an imposed restructure, in which they would have little say, proved to be a strong enough driver for people to let go of their deflection and scapegoat teddies and move to action.

While an external threat can get people to loosen their grip on scapegoat teddies, one can also use that teddy to influence those who have strong power and control needs. In this case, rather than get people to let go of the power teddy (which is very hard, if not impossible), one uses a scapegoat to create an *impression that their power and control has been taken away*.

To illustrate, let's say you are trying to get an idea sponsored or a project approved by someone who holds the power teddy tightly. All you might need to do is hint at the possibility that another party is trying to influence the decision. For example, by saying something like "HR seems to think that we can't do it this way." For the person attached to a power and control teddy, this creates an irrepressible urge to reassert control, to take their power teddy back so to speak. "Well they have another thing coming … it's my budget and I call the shots," is the sort of reply one could expect. Interestingly, your idea is far less important to them than their need to reassert control.

Ethically one has to be mindful of course, because not only are you handing out a scapegoat teddy which might misrepresent other people's actions and intentions, but you are also manipulating the recipient's perceptions. This highlights a general characteristic of any ambiguity management technique. Since these techniques are designed to manipulate intentions and consequent actions, it is clear that they can be used in both ethical and unethical ways. This is a critical point which we'll say a bit more about it later in this chapter and the next.

Divide and recombine

While the example above involved influencing an individual, things become trickier when multiple parties with differing interests and statuses are involved in decision making. Such scenarios can have a profound effect on trust and psychological safety, which is often driven by perceptions among stakeholders as to who calls the shots and who doesn't. In such situations, elephants in the room may remain unnamed because people do not feel safe to name them; some may suspect the motives and intentions of others, and some others may simply fear for their jobs.

A common approach used by facilitators in group scenarios—one that is very effective for synthesis and decision making—is the *divide and recombine* approach. The good thing about this technique is that you do not have to be an experienced facilitator to use it successfully. In brief it works as follows: at a certain point during a discussion or workshop, a large group is split randomly into smaller groups to answer a question or propose solutions. These groups are then brought back together to compare/contrast their solutions and insights, and identify common themes.

Smaller groups are, by definition, much more efficient than large groups when it comes to making decisions and taking action. Aside from that obvious benefit, it becomes harder for power players to disrupt or steer the outcomes because they can belong to only one group. Random assignment of people into these temporary groups removes the possibility of selection bias. Furthermore, if similar themes and insights emerge from different groups—as is often the case—it makes it harder for vested interests to ignore them.

As an example, Paul once facilitated a workshop for a very large public sector agency in which the outcome sought was a complete organisational redesign. The redesign extended all the way up to the executive team which consisted of 25 people, a number that was far too large to operate effectively. The problem was that participants of the workshop were all part of the current executive team and each one of them, naturally enough, felt *they* had earned the right to be there. Thus power teddies were being held tight and it was clear that any group discussion about the composition of the executive team would be difficult and likely end with the conclusion that everyone on the team was needed. While the Executive Director, who was new to the role, could have taken a dictatorial approach, the team consisted largely of experts who were both highly experienced and eminent. In other words, they were well-known in industry and well-connected. Given this, a dictatorial approach would have been risky for the newly appointed Executive Director because he might have come under considerable pressure if the situation turned adversarial.

After a day's work around goals, values and strategy had taken place, participants were randomly split into five groups and asked to spend thirty minutes discussing the ideal size of the executive, given what had emerged from the day. Each group was encouraged to leave the room to perform this task, the cover story being that the workshop was conducted in a location with great amenity, so they could get some fresh air and sunshine at the same time (while that was true, the real reason was to minimise inter-group influence).

Half an hour later, everyone reconvened and one-by-one, each group presented their conclusions as part of a plenary discussion. The ideal number for the executive team presented by the groups ranged from five to eleven members—a far cry from the original twenty-five. Now that each group had implicitly recognised the problem with the size of the team, the executive director had the mandate to make changes.

Shifting intentions...

In the last chapter, we mentioned that one of the strategies for dealing with wicked problems is to create the conditions that shift stakeholder intentions. Perhaps then, the ultimate power teddy removal strategy is to create conditions that enable parties to realise that a different approach is likely to yield a better outcome than any of the other alternatives. This could, for example, take the form of a KPI that rewards stakeholder engagement, or mandates collaborative behaviours.[36] As we showed earlier, two previously adversarial departments came together to pre-empt an organisational restructure in which both were likely to lose out. Such a change of conditions is also common in the global setting of corporate mergers, where two previous rival organisations magically find it in their interest to merge, especially if their common competitors have done so.

Indeed, organisations, unlike individuals, are driven more by interests than ideologies, and the former can be easier to change. We saw an example of this in the last chapter where the fossil fuel industry warmed towards climate change as renewables became more and more economically viable—this despite the fact that community attitudes to climate change are still (as we write these lines) somewhat more ambivalent. We do caution though ... in the event of a stakeholder changing their approach, the worst thing you can do is to treat it like a victory and gloat about it. Instead, reward them by handing out more teddies!

In this day and age of social media, there are many notable cases where online activism has gone viral, resulting in organisations rapidly

---

[36] In our previous book (Culmsee & Awati, 2013) we highlight a type of contract that is structured to reward collaborative behaviours

altering their strategies in response to public pressure. A good example of this was a disgruntled Australian Vodafone customer who created Vodafail.com, a complaints website and Twitter feed that went viral in 2011, enabling thousands of users (and frustrated Vodafone staff members) to vent their frustrations and dish dirt about poor service. This rapidly gained mainstream media attention and Vodafone was forced to respond, spending billions of dollars on network investment and increasing the number of Australian call centre staff. This bruising experience and resulting investment to address the problem paid off too. The Australian Telecommunications Industry Ombudsman reported that by late 2015, Vodafone Australia had gone from being the nation's most hated phone company to one with some of the lowest complaint levels in the industry. The Vodafail site was put into deep-freeze as traffic to the site dropped away.

The Vodafail example demonstrates an organisation changing its approach when it finds that it cannot control the entire playing field. There are also great examples where more subtle power teddy removal techniques resulted in non-cooperative stakeholders reassessing their approach to engagement. A notable one is the case of Hastings Pier in the UK[37]. The pier, located in East Sussex, England, was owned by an offshore company. It had long been in a state of disrepair and was eventually closed by local government because of safety concerns. A group of local people formed the Hastings Pier & White Rock Trust with the aim of buying the pier via a UK law that allows local councils to compulsorily purchase assets and transfer them to communities. Despite going through all the correct procedures required by the law and the council (such as developing business plans and demonstrating potential funds), it became increasingly apparent that the council had no *intention* of supporting a community owned and managed pier. They were instead holding out for a private sector organisation to come along and acquire the pier, a more comfortable scenario for them (community based acquisition of assets was seen by the council as being very risky).

---

[37] For a more detailed description of the Hastings Pier story, visit: http://www.jerichoroad.co.uk/2016/04/battle-hastings-pier/

The trust members felt they were being strung along despite having presented arguments that were in line with stated government and council policy. They realised they would have to take a different tack in order to change the council's perceptions. They decided to use a conveniently timed by-election to reframe the issue via a political campaign...

This was no small task. To change the position taken by the council, the trust had to energise jaded local residents into believing that the pier problem could actually be solved after years of trying. Without their support and passion, it would be difficult to convince political candidates that the pier was a vote winning issue. Rather than relying solely on the usual community engagement approach of distributing leaflets and conducting petitions, an indirect approach was used with great effect. Instead of "selling" the pier message directly, people were asked what they loved about the Hastings area, and what made them angry or frustrated. Many responses highlighted the seafront as being an important area, and that its *neglect* was a matter of great frustration. This in turn, led people to the realisation that the pier epitomised this neglect (picture a resident mulling over neglect and then suddenly saying "you're right you know ... the pier is really important!"). In effect, conditions were created whereby the community came to realise that the pier meant a lot.

With this scene set, it became possible to threaten some power teddies held by candidates vying for election. The point was for the candidates to realise that the pier was a critical issue that might stand between them being elected and losing out to another candidate. If the victorious candidate supported the pier, he or she would be able to influence an administration that had thus far, refused to engage on this issue. To achieve this, candidates were invited to a local school hall to participate in a debate and meet the community. This was well attended and very carefully stage-managed as then Trust Treasurer, Jess Steele, explained:

> "Just before the by-election we held a Candidates'
> Debate at the local primary school. Rather than giving
> the candidates a platform to give speeches on topics of

their choice, we managed the whole thing to focus on the pier—and establish the Trust's credibility as a future owner. This included shamelessly using my nine-year-old daughter and her friends in a dramatic presentation to explain why Hastings Pier is so strong and why it would cost £4m to demolish. We then gave the public a chance to question the candidates on any issues that concerned them. By the time we were done they were leaping up to sign the pledge that we had placed on an easel nearby!" (personal communication, April 25, 2016).

No matter who won the election, the trust now had commitment from all candidates who had directly experienced just how strongly the community felt about the pier. In fact, the very next day after the election was held, trust members were invited to the town hall to discuss the community acquisition of the pier with the council leadership and senior officers from the administration. Shortly after that, the council not only agreed to progress the community purchase of the pier, they allocated £200k for the costs. Suddenly the trust was in active partnership with the council—an amazing turnaround in a short space of time[38].

To sum up our journey so far, the key points on teddy bear removal illustrated by the previous examples include:

1. Teddy removal is about disrupting established defence mechanisms
2. No teddy is inherently good or bad, it's just that some go rogue. It is the context and the way in which the possessor uses it that determines its goodness or badness. Indeed, the teddies listed in Figure 7.4 may need to be removed at times while the teddies that feature in Figure 7.5 may need to be handed out (instead of being removed) in some situations.

---

[38] We have only told a small part of the Hastings Pier story here. Jess Steele was subsequently awarded an OBE for Services to Community Assets, largely from her role in the rescue of Hastings Pier from closure in 2006 to reopening in 2016

3. The subtle art of teddy removal is about shifting perceptions. Thus one should avoid focusing on the teddy by shifting focus on the outcome it is supposed to enable.

4. When it comes to making decisions and catalysing action, consider *divide and recombine* approaches. They can help reduce the influence of power and control teddies, and can streamline the decision making process.

5. Scapegoat teddies in the form of an external threat can be a useful way to move people to action ("we have a common enemy that means we might all lose...")

A common thread running through the case studies and examples we have covered is they establish *conditions that make it harder for any party to act unilaterally without undermining their own position*. This idea is not new. Elinor Ostrom, the Nobel laureate who we mentioned in Chapter 6, demonstrated how certain communities were able to manage common resources equitably and sustainably over the long term, despite different stakeholders having very different motives in relation to the resource. She pointed out that one of the key conditions required for this to happen *is reciprocity*, which refers to treating people the way you would want them to treat you. An obvious implication of reciprocity is that participants need to have willingness to give ground if they are expecting others to do so too.

Finally, all aspiring Ambiguity Jedis should note that the "do unto others as you would have them do unto you" aspect of reciprocity also has an important implication for the practice of ambiguity management. Put simply: if you are going to remove a teddy, you'd better be sure to have a replacement handy! This point segues nicely into our final ambiguity management tactic of swapping teddy bears.

Swapping teddy bears

Many of our readers would have encountered a scenario in which a three-year old child steadfastly refuses to let go of a toy, until a split-second later when it is tossed aside when a new toy is placed within reach. In the earlier section on handing out teddies, we warned against being a one-teddy wielder because different teddies are appropriate for different situations. There's another benefit too: if one has a lot of teddies handy, one can might be able to swap a teddy that has a negative influence with an alternative that is more likely to have a positive effect. In this section we look at how one can go about swapping teddies, an action that can help people *feel a sense of progress*—a condition that we feel is critical not only for maintaining a state of productive distress, but also for building reciprocity which Ostrom cited as being critical to collective action.

To begin with, we'll use a simple model to help explain the mysterious Jedi art of teddy substitution. Of all models we've described (and had fun with) so far in this book, this is one we urge you to take most seriously. Why? Because it has worked very well for us in diverse scenarios.

We'll start by using the table from Chapter 6 where we listed the different ways in which various luminaries have described problems that vary along a simple linear scale of ambiguity. This is shown in Figure 7.6

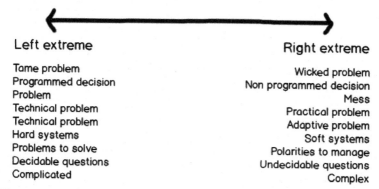

Left extreme	Right extreme
Tame problem	Wicked problem
Programmed decision	Non programmed decision
Problem	Mess
Technical problem	Practical problem
Technical problem	Adaptive problem
Hard systems	Soft systems
Problems to solve	Polarities to manage
Decidable questions	Undecidable questions
Complicated	Complex

Figure 7.6: The Ambiguity Scale

One aim of this model is to help determine where a problem lies along the spectrum of ambiguity. Is the problem technically complicated, yet the goal clear and relatively unambiguous? If so, chances are it is a tame or technical problem that lies towards the left of the figure.

Because the problem domain lies on the left side of the spectrum, it is best to use task/process-oriented tools such as those prescribed by project management methodologies. Get it done already!

But if the problem is on the right side of the spectrum, chances are the task/process oriented tools will actually *undermine the conditions* that enable these problems to be tackled effectively. Indeed, assuming the problem is well-formed and uncontroversial encourages the use of teddies—such as "Give me the facts", "All I need is a work instruction" or "Put up or shut up"—all of which are almost certainly wrong for the situation at hand. When facing problems like this, you are better off using sensemaking tools and techniques such as those described in our previous book (Culmsee & Awati, 2013).

Sensemaking tools work better because the right side problems are best tackled by *reflective* or dialogic modes of thinking—the kind of thinking that is needed when facts are ambiguous or disputed, and the relationship between cause and effect is unclear. In such situations, the role of communication goes way beyond simply conveying information (as in "give me the facts"). In fact, the primary purpose of communication is to *build relationships*. If one moves straight to the left side without such relationships being built first, the conditions of trust and reciprocity will never be established and the tools will be applied in a transactional, unthinking way. This not only risks them being used as weapons to quell genuine questions and independent thinking ("Standard says no"), it also risks falling into the trap of defensive behaviours that sidestep the real issues.

Speaking of tools, here's the second use for the model. When we ask people where a particular tool or approach sits on the spectrum, their responses tend to be remarkably consistent. For example, if one considers a work breakdown structure (WBS) used in project management—which is essentially a hierarchical list of project deliverables—most people will put it on the left side as shown in Figure 7.7. This is no surprise as a WBS is all about decomposing a large piece of work into its components, and decomposition is a key element of the analytical approach to problem-solving. Indeed, come to think of it, the vast majority of tools used in organisations are towards the left of the spectrum. Many people struggle to name tools that belong on the right side.

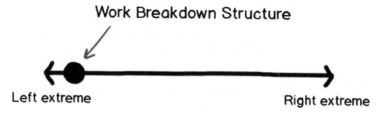

Figure 7.7: A Work Breakdown Structure as typically positioned on our problem spectrum

But despite their rarity in organisation land, such right side tools do exist and some of them are referred to as Problem Structuring Methods[39]. Open Space Technology is a good example of a right-side tool, although the word "Technology" is misleading. In (super) brief, Open Space is an approach to hosting meetings or workshops without any formal agenda. There is an overall purpose or theme to the workshop, but there is minimal prescribed structure. The approach relies on the participants organising themselves to identify and discuss the issues involved.

While this description does not do the method justice at all, it is easy enough to understand why most people would place it on the right hand side of the spectrum as shown in Figure 7.8 ... and also why some people, depending on their seesaw kid disposition, would have a really hard time dealing with it ("What? A talkfest with no agenda?? What is the outcome??? What is the point????").

---

[39] Our previous book covers various examples of sensemaking tools and problem structuring methods in detail.

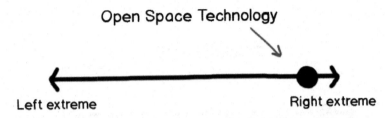

Figure 7.8: Open Space Technology as typically positioned on our problem spectrum

While the foregoing discussion is useful, we have not yet covered the key purpose of the model. Its real utility is that it gives us five core principles that help determine the approach, and therefore the teddies, that would work in any given situation:

1. The ideal starting point with problem solving is usually on the right (since most problems are initially ill-defined)
2. The ideal progression is usually from right to left (as the problem becomes clearer)
3. When there is divergence, move right (differences in perspectives cause a shift to the right)
4. When there is convergence, move left (consensus means that one can move to getting things done)
5. If you need to, trick people into adopting steps 1 and 4 by swapping out appropriate teddies

Points 1 to 4 would be enough in an ideal world where people can be convinced by logic alone. But in the messy world of reality where people are wedded to their own perceptions which are driven by which side the fat kid is on their mental seesaws, we need to invite (and gently coax) people who are on one side of the spectrum towards the other. Such a process of gentle cajoling might best be called *compassionate disruption*. Theorists must be nudged out of their right side comfort zone of theorizing so that they can start thinking about how to get stuff done, and action heroes must be slowed down so that they see and understand the big picture before they rush off to do stuff. Figure 7.9 illustrates the idea.

So how does one "compassionately disrupt"? Well ... that's what teddies are for. Consider our first example in this chapter: the linear management model of Figure 7.2 introduced at the start of a workshop as part of context setting. Such a model is rooted in "left-side" thinking. If our audience is action oriented, handing out this teddy will enable the facilitator leeway to ask "right side" questions that help to unpack the situation, surface assumptions and develop trust between stakeholders. As insights emerge, the group is pushed steadily left using more "convergent" approaches that seek decisions and commitment with the (often) ultimate intent of tasks, names, time and budgets assigned. Always remember the law of entropy ... if you stay using any one tool or approach too long, you run the risk of dissipating the energy you initially harness.

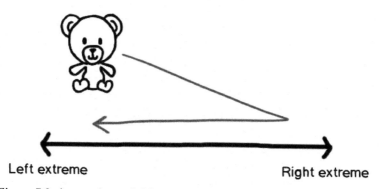

Hand out familiar left-side Teddy, sneak to the right, and push left

Left extreme　　　　　　　　**Right extreme**

Figure 7.9: A sample model for compassionate disruption

Powerful questions

Given that most people are familiar with left side tools such as checklists and processes, let's round out this chapter by examining some of these "right side" questions that can help facilitate a shared understanding of a situation and ultimately, *make it easier to move to the left* where things actually get done. Some might call these ambiguity Jedi Mind Tricks, but we prefer to call them Powerful Questions. You have already seen one of them—the "FUD Buster"—introduced in the section on teddy removal strategies. It is now time to meet a few other members of the powerful question family. In particular, we will cover:

- the "platitude buster" question;
- the "key focus area" question; and
- the "I told you so" question

First up, we are just going to be blunt and assert that many people *suck* at asking good questions (phew ... we feel better now and will stand by this assertion too). Organisation-land tends to be full of people who ask questions based on management models they have learnt in business school or read about in Forbes or Harvard Business Review. These include questions such as "What should our vision be?", "What should our quality strategy be?", "What are your requirements?" and "What are the risks?" While these sorts of questions are very important and definitely need to be answered, asking them at an early stage, usually elicits *less than useful answers unless the problem is very left sided and tame*. In fact, as counter-intuitive as it sounds, directly asked questions are *really hard to answer in wicked situations*. Moreover, asking them can end up amplifying ambiguity rather than delivering clarity. People often struggle to give meaningful answers and those given tend to be formulaic, missing important points that become obvious only in hindsight.

For example: asking "What should our quality strategy be?" immediately begs another question: "Well ... what do we mean by quality?" or "What is the definition of quality?" While this seems perfectly logical, we are now in serious danger of falling into *definition hell*—our term for the impossibility of getting a multidisciplinary group to agree on an up-front definition of a term because each specialist discipline has its own way of understanding the term. Indeed, in a wicked problem scenario it is difficult to get people on opposite sides of an issue to agree on *anything* upfront, let alone a definition.

The less obvious but bigger danger with jumping to the definition question is it encourages *paint-by-numbers thinking* that we mentioned in Chapter 1. Specifically, those who base their definition off a pre-existing model run the risk of:

- overlooking critical features that are specific to the situation at hand (i.e. they assume the paint-by-numbers model sufficiently describes the particular organisation's reality); and
- applying factors that are irrelevant (by assuming they have to "paint all the numbered areas" of the chosen model up-front).

Remember, we are talking about right-side situations that have elements of wickedness. If you have assessed the situation to be a tame or technical problem, we say "Go for it! Definitionise to your heart's content!"

In wicked situations however, a more effective approach is to allow a definition to *emerge* by asking *what difference it would make if we had the thing people are seeking to define*. As an example:

"What is the definition of governance?"

should be reframed as:

"If we really (and I mean really) had successful governance, how would things be different to now?"

We call this powerful question the platitude buster question, and it has a number of benefits:

1. It refocuses the group's attention on the desired end state rather than the means to get there.
2. It invites answers from everyone in the group, and is not bound by any imposed model defined up-front.
3. It fosters a shared understanding of the current situation by eliciting multiple viewpoints, thus building an appreciation of the specific context surrounding the issue.

4. It invites answers like "Increased X", "Eliminating Y" or "Decreasing Z". These are useful because it gives insight into potential ways in which one can measure success. Further, this provides an excellent segue into other activities that are aimed at defining key performance indicators (KPIs) to quantify success (Can you see how this moves things toward the left of Figure 7.9?).

5. The need for formal definitions has been largely mitigated because a working model has been socially constructed through collaborative sensemaking. At this point, it might be useful to use existing supermodels or definitions to check that the working model is sensible. A side benefit is that this is a nice way to hand a teddy to fans of models or definitions.

So why do we call this question the "platitude buster"? Simple ... because it also works on every one of those dodgy management platitudes like "best practice collaboration", "organisational excellence" or "big data analytics". For example, instead of asking "What do we mean by big data analytics?" one asks "If we had big data analytics, how would things be different to now?"

Neat eh? Next time you are given a juicy management platitude you can unpack what it actually means by focusing on what it is supposed to achieve instead of getting bogged down in an unproductive definition-fest.

The general platitude buster question archetype is along the lines of:

> "If you had [insert platitude here], how would things be different to now?"

Although you can use pretty much anything in the placeholder, you will find it particularly useful to ask this question whenever you feel a group is not aligned on a topic, or are blindly chasing a platitude or fad.

It is important to note that you may need to hand out a teddy before asking the platitude buster question. This is to mitigate any anxiety felt by those who thrive on definitions. Indeed, you might be surprised just how many people can't handle discussing a topic without defining it first...

Paul once co-facilitated an all-day strategic planning workshop involving over fifty academics, representing a dozen organisations. All those present worked in areas relating to sustainability development. Paul and his colleague knew they were dealing with an audience who were strong "need for cognition" types, and the teddy bear holders would want to begin with an up-front definition of "sustainability" (when you think about it, a definition teddy serves a similar anxiety reduction need that "Just give me a work instruction" teddy does for action heroes).

The problem in this case was that the *"Give me a definition"* teddy would destroy the conditions needed for collective action because some organisations did not recognise the legitimacy of others in the room. For example, some participants felt that there was no such thing as *sustainable mining*, yet one of the organisations present was dedicated to mining sustainability. Accordingly, the day was designed to avoid a definition debate up front by handing out an alternate *legitimiser* teddy: the facilitators mentioned that the workshop approach was specifically designed for wicked problems and was backed up with liberal dollop of terminology from complexity theory[40]. It was thought that the "wicked problem" legitimiser teddy, wrapped in a garb of complexity theory, would address the cognitive needs of the academically oriented audience to the point where they would no longer insist on definitions. However, a fallback was designed just in case ... to have some time allocated for a definition discussion in the late afternoon, rather than first thing in the morning.

In the actual workshop, the predictable happened. Within minutes of starting, it was suggested by participants that a good start to the day would be a definition of sustainability. Fortunately, the substitute teddy handed out was enough to forestall this discussion. But not all participants' anxieties were sufficiently reduced. During the lunch break, one participant sought reassurance that the definition discussion would

---

[40] See https://en.wikipedia.org/wiki/Complex_systems or https://en.wikipedia.org/wiki/Complex_adaptive_system for more detail on complexity topics

indeed happen, so once most of the strategic priorities had been worked out, the discussion commenced. Predictably, it did not get very far because, academics being academics, like nothing more than a catfight over definitions. Fortunately, the disagreements in the afternoon's discussion did not derail the work that was done earlier in the day. Sometimes teddies serve as useful verbal punching bags—they allow people to let off intellectual steam without coming in the way of them doing productive work.

Go indirect first...

Platitudes and "definition hell" are not the only examples of the problems with asking direct questions in wicked situations. Another good example is around identifying the *scope and risks of an initiative*. The obvious questions to ask here are "What is the scope for this initiative?" and "What are the risks?" While these will certainly identify some scope elements and risks, experience suggests that augmenting the direct questions with less direct ones, results in richer and more meaningful answers.

For matters relating to scope, a useful question we call the "key focus area question" is:

> "What aspects of [insert problem or issue here] should we be considering?"

The use of the word like "aspects" or "elements" is deliberate. It is neutrally framed and therefore admits a wider variety of viewpoints than questions like "What are the issues?" The problem with the latter question, and similar ones such as "What are the risks?" is that they are framed in negative terms. This prompts respondents to think in terms of issues or risks rather than a broader perspective that considers all aspects of the matter being discussed. Conversely, if one were to ask "What are the opportunities?" the group would focus on positive aspects, thereby running the risk that those ever-present elephants in the room remain unnamed.

The important thing to note with this question is that focus areas tend to *emerge* via recurring themes rather than being named up front. In other words, after the initial answers are given, participants usually start to see deeper issues and make comments like "What this really is about is…" and name an underlying theme. It is therefore critically important to be attuned to potential emerging themes! The Hastings Pier is a brilliant example of this. In that case, residents were not asked to save the pier, but asked what frustrated them the most, and the pier emerged as a key theme.

Finally, when it comes to specifically identifying risks, we recommend using the "I told you so" powerful question or its variants. Examples variants of this question include:

- What keeps you up at night regarding [insert problem or issue here]?
- If things go bad 6 months from now and you said "See, I told you so…" what would the "I told you so" be?
- What are your concerns with [insert action here]?

This question deliberately pokes at ambiguity intolerance and social defences. As we learnt in Chapter 3, it has long been known that different regions of the human brain are activated when people are faced with ambiguous choices versus logical choices. Ambiguity is processed in the more primal parts of the brain that also regulate emotions. The obvious question: "What are the risks?" is framed in a way that it is processed in the logical part of the brain. It will identify all sorts of interesting risks that could logically happen, but a lot more can be revealed if you also ask "and what is keeping you up at night about this?" The latter question seeks to draw out anxiety-laden responses because it reminds people about the fears they may have about the initiative. This means that it is more likely to trigger responses from the primal parts of the brain as well.

The framing of risk related questions in a personalised manner is therefore better because it requires people to engage with the issues being discussed in a more visceral way. This is a good thing because participants are then induced to view the issue through perspectives other than a purely fact-based one.

Wielding the force...

Now that you have taken a journey through a day in the life of an ambiguity Jedi, you might have started to recognise other teddy bears that your colleagues clutch to their chest on a daily basis. You might also have a heap of other ambiguity manipulation Jedi tricks and powerful questions that we haven't mentioned. There is a good reason for this: the art of management is a tacit craft. Just as it's impossible to learn to play guitar by reading a book, you need to forge your own path based on your experiences.

As we have mentioned earlier, the careful reader may also have noticed that the art of ambiguity management via teddy bears (or any other means) is essentially about *manipulation*. This means that it has significant ethical implications, a point we'll discuss in the next chapter. For now, we will close this chapter with a warning...

If people realise they are being manipulated, they will invariably change their behaviours. This implies that nothing we have said in this chapter is guaranteed to work for you. A large part of whether it does or doesn't depends on your tacit appreciation of the situation, your choice of teddy bears and the subtlety with which you hand, take away or swap them out. We hope that if you have taken to heart what we've said so far—starting from paint-by-numbers models to management fads and physics envy—you will understand why this is (and has to be) so. Humans do not behave as predictably as molecules do, so shaping conditions via teddy-bear management can never have the predictability of a science. Indeed, as we will discuss in the final chapter, it is precisely for this reason that the art of managing ambiguity is necessarily an indirect or oblique one—and consequently is more art than science.

Coda

It Ends With Us

"We have met the enemy, and they are us"

—Walt Kelly (paraphrased)

A recap

Now that we're almost at the end of this book, it is worth taking some time to recapitulate our journey through ambiguity. We think the best way to begin this is by fessing up to an important point that we have carefully avoided mentioning thus far.

When we started writing this book a couple of years ago, we had absolutely no idea that it would end up being about ambiguity management. Like our first book, we knew we had something to say about the practice of management, but had little idea that it would end up where it did. Indeed, when we started on Chapter 1—in which we introduced you to our paint-by-numbers Mona Lisa—our intent was to focus on the shortcomings of *causal* models in management, i.e. models claiming that if you do this (the cause) then you will get certain specific results (the effect) .

As we progressed, we realised that the point is not so much that causal models are flawed, but that humans seem to have a deep need to believe in them. One could go so far as to say that humans are *hardwired* to seek causal connections between events. Much of daily activity hinges on this simple fact. For example, I catch the bus at 7:00 am (cause) because I want to get to work by 7:30 (effect), my boss gives me a bonus (cause) because he thinks it will make me feel appreciated (effect) and so on. If one thinks about it, the evolution of management over the last century and a half, has largely been about trying to find better ways (causes) to achieve desirable results (effects).

The problem is this task is nowhere as near as straightforward as the supermodels seem to suggest...

In Chapter 2, we saw that the history of management has been characterised by oscillations between two dominant paradigms: process-oriented and people-focused. At any given time, one paradigm dominates, and it is the socioeconomic zeitgeist that determines the dominant one. This makes sense when you consider that in times of plenty, the focus is on people because it is easy for people to switch jobs if they perceive they're being short-changed. But in hard times, the focus tends to be on process since the organisation needs to find ways to improve efficiency and productivity. One of the consequences of this oscillation between two extremes is that most management techniques have a short shelf life—they tend to be fads (at best!) rather than universal truths. Indeed, as the history of scientific management from Taylor through to the Lean and Stoos movements showed, the same ideas keep popping up every decade or two, albeit in a morphed form.

The interesting thing is that the two paradigms are mutually exclusive in practice. In Chapter 3, we elaborated on this point by discussing how the oscillations in management theory are mirrored in our mental make-up. Imaging studies have shown, quite unambiguously, that at any given time an individual can either be task-oriented (logical) or people-oriented (emotionally aware), but rarely both at the same time. Put simply, the more logical and task oriented one is in their thinking, the less empathetic and vice-versa. To be sure, individuals have innate preferences for one mode of thinking over the other, and in times of stress, revert to their preferred mode. However, it appears very difficult to be logical and emotionally aware concurrently. The oscillation between logic and emotion at the level of the discipline of management is replicated on a smaller scale within the head of every manager!

This by itself is not necessarily a problem. The real issue is that in most practical situations it is not obvious as to which mode of thinking or even which model is appropriate.

Why? The one-word answer is *ambiguity*.

The term *ambiguity* made its debut in Chapter 3, where we made the point that most decisions—both in life and work—have to be made under conditions of ambiguity. In that chapter, we discussed research in neuroscience, showing that ambiguity is processed in the areas of the brain that regulate emotional responses. Among other things, this explains why people get anxious when ambiguity is high, which in turn triggers a flight to safety to the comfort of the familiar. For those in such situations, the "do-this-and-you-will-get-that" certainty of causal management models offer a highly seductive ambiguity coping mechanism because of the promise of certainty and control it offers. But there is a problem. While anxiety might be reduced in the short term, it is often a mirage because such apparently rational "solutions" do not solve the problem. Worse, they often lead to defensive behaviours that preclude genuine learning and end up being self-defeating rituals. We called this *anti-learning*.

We expanded on *ambiguity intolerance* in Chapter 4 by examining the reasons why smart people do dumb things. We looked at the all-important distinction between *intelligence* and *rationality*, the latter being immeasurably more important in situations of uncertainty. Rational thinking requires a person to be able to *reflect* on a situation, as well as his or her own opinions and reactions to it, in a critical manner. This is a rare skill for two reasons. Firstly, humans tend to be cognitive misers—many of us are consciously and subconsciously loath to put in the additional effort required to think rationally. Secondly, and perhaps more insidiously, there are two issues associated with mindware—the mental tools that help in assessing decision problems. The first issue is called the *mindware gap*, where people are not aware of the tools they need to tackle decision problems. The second is the problem of *contaminated mindware*, where tools or models being used are flawed.

We rounded out the first part of the book by revisiting the notion of causality in management in Chapter 5. In particular, we pointed out that management—and indeed most of the "soft sciences"—suffer from *physics envy*. That is, those who work in the soft sciences aspire to reach the lofty heights of theoretical and experimental rigour routinely achieved by physicists. Unfortunately, this is an impossible task because these disciplines deal with conglomerations of humans rather than molecules. The behaviour of atoms can be reduced to simple rules, whereas that of individual humans, for the most part, cannot. We then pointed out that when dealing with ambiguous situations, it may be more fruitful to include indirect approaches that focus on *creating the conditions that are conducive to meaningful collaboration*, rather than attempting to influence individuals by *imposing* attractive, but superficial management models.

Chapters 1 through 5 set the stage for part 2, which is largely about the *art of ambiguity management*. In Chapter 6, we made the notion of ambiguity more precise via the concept of problem wickedness. We made the point that in most organisational scenarios, ambiguity arises from differences in perspectives about the "facts" around a problem. This leads to a diversity of opinions as to what the problem *is*, let alone how it should be solved. In such situations, the best one can do is create the conditions for collaboration and creativity, and let the group work out its own solution.

Finally, in Chapter 7, we pointed out that ambiguity by itself is neither good nor bad. A useful metaphor is to think of it is as a force that can be harnessed in positive or negative ways—akin to The Force in the Star Wars series of movies. Much of Chapter 7 is about simple tools that can be used to harness this force in positive ways. The tools are based on the notion of transition objects that we first mentioned in Chapter 3. In essence, ambiguity management—via teddy bears or any other method—is about containing anxiety in situations where it is too high or, conversely, ramping it up just enough to move people to take action. It is the delicate art of getting people to *shift* their mode of thinking, *but in a way that is unobtrusive*. The latter point is so important that it merits a section of its own...

The power and paradox of obliquity

When one steps back and looks at a thread running through the last chapter (and indeed, much of the book), a recurrent theme emerges: the notion of *obliquity*—that some goals are best pursued in an indirect way. This idea is far from new. For example, according to Zen Buddhism, enlightenment is attained not by deliberate attempts to achieve it, but by meditation (zazen) *with no expectation of enlightenment* (Suzuki, 1973). Similarly, people seeking "happiness" tend not to be as happy as those who find contentment, if not happiness, via the pursuit of other goals. Although that may sound a bit hippie and far removed from practical concerns, John Kay (2011) pointed out that obliquity has very practical implications. In a 1998 lecture at Oxford University, he stated:

> "I do not recommend that you read Bill Gates' recent book any more than I recommend Al Dunlap's. But if you do read them both, you should notice the contrast. Gates' is entitled The Road Ahead, while Dunlap's is called Mean Business. Gates is enthused by what

businesses he might set up, Dunlap by those he might close down. But, above all, you will learn that while Dunlap's primary concern is money, Gates is basically an interest in computers. Yet it is Gates, not Dunlap, who is the richest man in America. I call this paradox the principle of obliquity. It says that some objectives are best pursued indirectly" (Kay J. , 2009).

Kay asserts that the most profitable companies tend not to be the most profit-oriented, and cites examples of organisations whose direct focus on shareholder returns was self-defeating. Jack Welch (Guerrera, 2009) echoed this sentiment when asked in a Financial Times interview what he thought of "shareholder value" as a strategy. He stated that it was the "dumbest idea in the world," a comment that sent the MBA world into meltdown. Elaborating a few weeks later, he said: (emphasis ours)

"You would never tell your employees, 'Shareholder value is our strategy.' That's not a strategy you can touch. That's not a strategy that helps you know what to do when you come to work every day. It doesn't energize or motivate anyone. So basically my point is, *increasing the value of your company in both the short and long term is an outcome of the implementation of successful strategies*" (Welch, 2009).

We believe the obliquity principle also applies to ambiguity management. The fact is, any new situation or problem faced by an organisation is imbued with ambiguity. As a consequence, the actions to be taken are far from obvious because the problem itself is not well understood. What is needed before jumping to action is to *make sense of the situation* and formulate the problem that needs to be solved (if there is indeed a problem at all). Strangely enough, indirect approaches supported by the appropriate teddy bears seem to work better than direct actions. This is because *they not only reduce anxiety associated with change, but also reduce pressure, thereby creating an environment that enables people to perceive subtle contextual elements that tend to remain hidden in high-pressure situations.*

Sensemaking as a skill...

Most people are very good at solving problems that are *well-defined*. This is no surprise, since most educational programs, right from school, university and through to the world of work, focuses on teaching us the skills required to solve problems. Regardless of the specific technique used, the process is essentially a logical or analytical one. It goes something like this:

- Gather information about the problem.
- Analyse the information.
- Formulate candidate solutions.
- Implement the solution of choice.

This so-called GAFI method is *direct* in that it tackles the problem head-on. It works by breaking problems down into manageable parts, solving each of the parts separately and then assembling these into a solution. The method works very well for most scientific and engineering problems, even one as complicated as sending a spacecraft to Saturn. Indeed, it is so successful that it underpins much of science and modern technology.

However, as we have highlighted in this book, there is a serious (mindware) gap in the GAFI method. It assumes that problems are given: it does not tell us how to formulate problems—an issue that is particularly acute in complex or wicked situations. The art of *taking problems from complex or wicked situations* is what *sensemaking* is all about. Unlike analytical thinking, which is purely logical, sensemaking involves skills such as collaboration, imagination and above all, *a healthy tolerance for ambiguity*. It is an art that is absolutely essential for surviving ... no, *thriving*, in the increasingly complex world of the 21st century.

These two modes of thinking, *sensemaking* and *analytical*, are as different as chalk and cheese but both are necessary for a successful outcome. We like to think of them as lying at opposite ends of a spectrum of thinking styles as shown in Figure 8.1. As discussed in the last chapter, when approaching an ambiguous situation, one should begin at the sensemaking end and move towards the analytical end as one understands the situation better. Unfortunately, time pressures—not to mention mindware gaps, fetishes and defensive behaviours—in corporate environments, often force managers and employees into analytical mode without a full appreciation of the situation they are in. Typically, this results in less than optimal outcomes. The ambiguity management techniques discussed in this book, together with the practical sensemaking methods presented in our previous one (Culmsee and Awati 2013) are intended to address this issue. When used in tandem, they can help groups deal with ambiguous situations in highly productive ways.

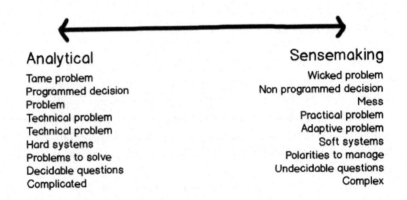

Figure 8.1: Analytics and Sensemaking

Towards a holding environment?

In our previous book, we developed the notion of a *holding environment,* which we defined as an environment that fosters *open dialogue* (also see

Culmsee & Awati, 2012)—the kind of discussion that occurs when the following conditions[41] are met:

- **Inclusion:** all affected stakeholders are included in the dialogue.
- **Autonomy:** all participants are able to present their viewpoints and debate those of others independently.
- **Empathy:** participants are willing to listen to viewpoints that may be different from theirs and make the effort to understand them.
- **Power neutrality:** differences in status or authority levels do not affect the discussion.
- **Transparency:** participants are completely honest when presenting their views or discussing those of others.

We also mentioned that three of these conditions—inclusion, autonomy and power neutrality—are under management control, i.e. management can create these conditions if they wish to. The remaining two conditions, empathy and transparency, are determined by individual intent. There's not much management can do if people do not wish to be transparent or empathetic.

But all is not lost … the techniques discussed in Chapter 7 are actually aimed at addressing (or to put it more crassly, *manipulating*) individual intentions under conditions of ambiguity. The use of teddy bears reduces or ramps up anxiety to a point where people's intentions *can* be influenced. We'd go so far as to say that the best managers understand what makes their people tick to the point where they can shift intentions through subtle interventions that often involve a teddy bear or two. Once anxiety is reduced, people often end up being more open (transparency) and willing to listen to others (empathy), thus meeting those elusive conditions that are required in order to make progress on wicked problems.

---

[41] Note, once again, that open dialogue cannot be "created" or "caused", one can only set up the right conditions and hope for the best.

Paul Culmsee and Kailash Awati

The price of collaboration (the one teddy that can ruin it all)

We have spent a lot of time talking about intention and how to shift it in this book, but there is one teddy bear we have deliberately *not* mentioned so far. One that, if it goes rogue, will stop even the most genuine intentions cold. Here is the teddy…

Figure 8.2: The one teddy that can ruin it all

Huh? This is a plain old teddy, so what are we getting at?

Collaboration is *hard* because it requires us to not only be open to new ideas, but also to accept that it inevitably means that our own dearly held ideas will be critically scrutinised by others. Therefore, a prerequisite for the success of any collaborative effort is that every individual must realise that criticisms arising from such scrutiny are not personal attacks, but genuine attempts to achieve better outcomes.

The price of collaboration therefore, is that one has to be willing to let one's ideas go … or even die. Many people struggle with this because they are unable to distinguish themselves from their ideas. The needed attitude is best summed up by the phrase "you are not your idea". This is hard to live up to. We have observed many people who, despite being keen advocates of collaborative approaches, are simply unable to let their ideas go. If you ever find yourself in such a situation, remember that

182

bringing a "collaborative" group together to buy-in to a solution that you have pre-supposed is not collaboration, but coercion.

The teddies such people so desperately cling on to are themselves.

The ethics of ambiguity management

In case it isn't obvious already, one of the characteristics of wicked problems is that they cannot be addressed by logic alone. This is because the application of logical methods presumes that everyone agrees on *what the problem is* as well as the *facts surrounding the problem.* Neither of these conditions are fulfilled for wicked problems.

In practical terms this means a manager faced with a wicked situation will invariably have to be guided by considerations other than logic. All these other considerations, whatever they may be, must reframe the problem so as to render it tractable. Above all, such a reframing involves a shift in perspective. The ambiguity management techniques outlined in the previous chapter serve to reduce anxiety to a point where those in the group can achieve such a shift without freaking out and reverting to the usual defensive teddies that end up doing more harm than good.

This brings up an important point which we have alluded to earlier. The techniques discussed in this and our previous book ought not to be used to frame the problem in a way that is based on the interests of a specific group while ignoring others. Indeed, the appropriate frame is one that takes into account the *entire* spectrum of interests and opinions relating to the problem.

In reality however, *the choice of frame is entirely up to the person who wields power in the room*—usually the most senior manager. Although such a manager may frame his or her decision as a logical one, it is really an ethical matter because it is entirely up to him or her as to whether or not to let people in the group make their choices without pressure. Indeed, the choices made in such situations are hugely influenced by the type of questions asked when the discussion is initiated. In particular, questions can be either authentic or inauthentic. With the former, those asking questions are genuinely seeking answers. With the latter, the questions are loaded, they are framed by interests and intent of the askers.

The crucial implication of the above is that since wicked issues cannot be decided by logic alone, managers actually have considerable freedom in that they are free to decide how to approach a problem. An implication of this is that *the choice made by the senior manager in a wicked situation reveals more about the manager than the problem because it is made on the basis of the manager's beliefs rather than objective truths.* This places a colossal responsibility on managers, so much so that modern management practice has provided numerous rogue teddies to sidestep it. As the polymath Heinz von Foerster (2003) put it:

> "With much ingenuity and imagination, mechanisms have been contrived by which one can bypass this awesome burden. With hierarchies, entire institutions have been built where it is impossible to localize responsibility. Everyone in such a system can say: 'I was told to do X.'
>
> [For example] On the political stage we hear more and more the phrase of Pontius Pilate: 'I have no choice but X.' In other words, 'Don't make me responsible for X, blame others.' This apparently replaces: 'Among the many choices I had, I decided on X.' " (p. 293).

Such I-have-no-choice decisions are often clothed in a garb of objectivity. As Foerster continued:

> "Objectivity requires that the properties of the observer do not entire the description of his or her observations. With this removed, the observer is reduced to a copying machine, and the notion of responsibility successfully juggled away" (p. 293).

The mechanisms of decision-making and problem-solving in organisations enable ... no, *encourage* managers to avoid the burden of responsibility rather than accept it. "Sorry, but it is business" or "I'm just following orders" are two common "soldier teddy" phrases that flag such avoidance. From personal experience, we are painfully aware of how easy it is to sweep ethical issues out of one's field of vision when dealing with wicked problems, and that important business decisions invariably involve such issues.

It all starts with us ... and ends with us too

We began our previous book with an analogy between employees in an organisation and the old-fashioned marble board game (now available on all smartphones). The aim of the game is to navigate a marble through a maze by tilting the board appropriately, while avoiding hazards (holes) along the way. In real life, the holes are akin to things that tend to have a negative effect on the employee's sense of well-being ... which is why he or she would prefer to avoid them.

Navigating a single marble through the maze is easy enough, but the game gets complicated once there are multiple marbles. One complicating factor is that different people fear different things: a hazard for Tom is not necessarily one for Jennifer. Another is that the organisation has its own sense of what is good and what is not (its own hazards), and its hazards are quite likely to be different from those of rank and file employees.

Although those who run the organisation have the power to decide which way the board is tilted, the individual marbles have a mind of their own and can choose how they respond to the tilt. If the tilt is counter to their sense of well-being, they are likely to resist—overtly if they can and covertly if they can't. This is why it is so critical to manage ambiguity upfront. It addresses individual concerns about perceived hazards and what can be done to alleviate them.

It is as we wrote in our previous book:

> "While this is a book about organisations ... the marble game metaphor is useful to illustrate that *it all starts with us [the individual employees in the organisation]*."

To this we would now add that it ends with individual employees too, for it is their attitudes to ambiguity that determine their intentions and ultimately, the outcomes that managers so dearly wish to influence.

References

Ackoff, R., & Emery, F. (2005). *On purposeful systems: An interdisciplinary analysis of individual and social behavior as a system of purposeful events.* New Brunwick: Transaction Publishers.

Aczel, B., Bago, B., Szollosi, A., Foldes, A., & Lukacs, B. (2015). Measuring Individual Differences in Decision Biases: Methodological Considerations. *Frontiers in Psychology.*

Argyris, C. (1990). *Overcoming organizational defenses.* Boston, MA: Allyn and Bacon.

Australian Public Service Commission. (2007). *Tackling Wicked Problems: A Public Policy Perspective.* Retrieved May 29, 2016, from Australian Public Service Commission: http://www.apsc.gov.au/__data/assets/pdf_file/0005/6386/wickedproblems.pdf

Bad Science: A Resouce Book. (1993, March 26). Retrieved May 29, 2016, from Truth Tobacco Smoking Documents: https://www.industrydocumentslibrary.ucsf.edu/tobacco/docs/#id=qmcj0065

Bain, A. (1998). Social defenses against organizational learning. *Human Relations, 51*(3), 413.

Balleine, B., Delgado, M., & Hikosaka, O. (2007). The role of the dorsal striatum in reward and decision-making. *The Journal of Neuroscience, 27*(31), 8161–8165.

Barley, S. R., & Kunda, G. (1992). Design and Devotion: Surges of Rational and Normative Ideologies of Control in Managerial DIscourse. *Administrative Science Quarterly, 37*(3), 363-399.

Bateson, G., Jackson, D., Haley, J., & Weakland, J. (1956). Towards a Theory of Schizophrenia. *Behavioral Science, 1*(4), 251-254.

Baumeister, R. F., & Leary, M. R. (1995). need to belong: Desire for interpersonal attachments as a fundamental human motivation. *Psychological Bulletin, 117*(3), 497-529.

Better Markets. (2012, September 5). *The Cost of The Wall Street-caused financial Collapse and Ongoing Economic Crisis is More Than $12.8*

Trillion. Retrieved from Better Markets: https://www.bettermarkets.com/sites/default/files/Cost%20O f%20The%20Crisis_0.pdf

Birnbaum, R. (2000). *Management fads in higher education: Where they come from, what they do, why they fail.* San Francisco: Jossey-Bass.

Bochner, S. (1965). Defining intolerance of ambiguity. *psychological record, 15*(3), 393.

Box, G. (1979). Robustness in the strategy of scientific model building. In R. Launer, & G. Wilkinson (Eds.), *Robustness in Statistics* (pp. 201-236). Academic Press.

Boyatzis, R., Rochford, K., & Jack, A. (2014). Antagonistic neural networks underlying differentiated leadership roles. *Front. Hum. Neurosci, 8*(114).

Capstick, S., Whitmarsh, L., Poortinga, W., Pidgeon, N., & Upham, P. (2015). International trends in public perceptions of climate change over the past quarter century. *WIREs Clim Change.*

Chia, R., & Holt, R. (2008). The Nature of Knowledge in University Business Schools. *Academy of Management Learning & Education, 7*(4), 471-486.

Clarke, K. A., & Primo, D. M. (2012, March 30). *Overcoming 'Physics Envy'.* Retrieved from New York Times: http://www.nytimes.com/2012/04/01/opinion/sunday/the-social-sciences-physics-envy.html

Cohen, A. R., Stotland, E., & Wolfe, D. (1955). An experimental investigation of need for cognition. *Journal of Abnormal and Social Psychology, 51*(2), 291.

Collopy, F. (2009, July 6). *Lessons Learned — Why the Failure of Systems Thinking Should Inform the Future of Design Thinking.* Retrieved from FastCompany: http://www.fastcompany.com/1291598/lessons-learned-why-failure-systems-thinking-should-inform-future-design-thinking

Conklin, J. (2005). *Dialogue mapping: Building shared understanding of wicked problems.* John Wiley & Sons, Inc.

Cook, J., Nuccitelli, D., Green, S. A., Richardson, M., Winkler, B., Painting, R., . . . Skuce, A. (2013). Quantifying the consensus on anthropogenic global warming in the scientific literature. *Environmental Research Letters, 8*(2).

Culmsee, P., & Awati, K. (2012). Towards a holding environment: building shared understanding and commitment in projects. *International Journal of Managing Projects in Business, 5*(3), 528-548.

Culmsee, P., & Awati, K. (2013). *The Heretic's Guide to Best Practices: The Reality of Managing Complex Problems in Organisations.* iUniverse Star.

Dankbaar, B. (1997). Lean Production: Denial, Confirmation or Extension of Sociotechnical Systems Design? *Human Relations, 50*(5), 567-583.

Deci, E. L., & Ryan, R. M. (2008). Self-determination theory: A macrotheory of human motivation, development, and health. *Canadian Psychology/Psychologie canadienne, 49*(3), 182.

Digital Taylorism: A modern version of "scientific management" threatens to dehumanise the workplace. (2015, September 10). *Economist.*

Ellis, G., & Silk, J. (2014). Scientific method: Defend the integrity of physics. *Nature,* 321.

Ellsberg, D. (1961). Risk, Ambiguity, and the Savage Axioms. *The Quarterly Journal of Economics, 75*(4), 643-669.

Feldman Barrett, L. (2015, September 1). *Psychology Is Not in Crisis.* Retrieved from New York Times: http://www.nytimes.com/2015/09/01/opinion/psychology-is-not-in-crisis.html

Fleischman, R. K. (2000). Completing the triangle: Taylorism and the paradigms. *Accounting, Auditing & Accountability Journal, 13*(5), 597-624.

Foerster, H. v. (2003). Ethics and Second Order Cybernetics. In *Understanding understanding* (pp. 287-304). New York: Springer.

Frank, A., & Glieser, M. (2015, June 5). *A Crisis at the Edge of Physics.* Retrieved from New York Times: http://www.nytimes.com/2015/06/07/opinion/a-crisis-at-the-edge-of-physics.html

Frey, D. (2002, December 8). How Green Is BP? *New York Times Magazine.*

Frey, R., McNeil, A. J., & Nyfeler, M. (2001). Copulas and credit models. *Risk, 10*(111114.10).

Ghoshal, S. (2005). Bad Management Theories Are Destroying Good Management Practices. *Academy of Management, Learning and Education, 4*(1), 75-91.

Goldratt, E. (1990). *The Haystack Syndrome: Sifting Information out of the Data Ocean*. Great Barrington, MA: North River Press.

Guerrera, F. (2009, March 13). *Welch denounces corporate obsessions.* Retrieved from Financial Times: http://www.ft.com/cms/s/0/3ca8ec2e-0f70-11de-ba10-0000779fd2ac.html?ft_site=falcon&desktop=true

Hackman, R. (2004). What makes for a great team? *APA Science Briefs, 18*.

Hackman, R. (2012). From causes to conditions in group research. *Journal of Organizational Behavior*, 428-444.

Hambrick, D. C. (2007). The Field of Managagement's Devotion to Theory: Too Much of a Good Thing? *Academy of Management Journal, 50*(6), 1346-1352.

Harari, O. (1997). Ten reasons why TQM does not work. *Management review, 86*(1), 38.

Herndon, T., Ash, M., & Pollin, R. (2013). Does High Public Debt Consistently Stifle Economic Growth? A Critique of Reinhart and Rogoff. *Cambridge Journal of Economics, 38*(2), 257-279.

Hsu, M. (2004, June 9). Ambiguity Aversion in the Brain. *Caltech Working Paper*. Pasadena, CA, USA. Retrieved from https://www.researchgate.net/profile/Ming_Hsu4/publication/251847916_Ambiguity_Aversion_in_the_Brain/links/55f7114d08ae07629dbd63d6.pdf

Hsu, M., Bhatt, M., Adolphs, R., Tranel, D., & Camerer, C. (2005). Neural Systems Responding to Degrees of Uncertainty in Human Decision-Making. *Science 310*(5754), 1680-1683.

Jost, J. T., Kruglanski, A. W., Glaser, J., & Sulloway, F. J. (2003). Political Conservatism as Motivated Social Cognition. *Psychological Bulletin*, 339-375.

Kahneman, D. (2002). Maps of bounded rationality: A perspective on intuitive judgment and choice. *Nobel prize lecture, 8*, pp. 351-401.

Kahneman, D. (2011). *Thinking, fast and slow*. Macmillan.

Kahneman, D. (2014). *A New Etiquette for Replication.* Retrieved from https://www.scribd.com: https://www.scribd.com/doc/225285909/Kahneman-Commentary

Kahneman, D., & Smith, V. (2002). Foundations of behavioral and experimental economics. *Nobel Prize in Economics Documents.*

Kay, J. (2009). The role of business in society. John Kay. Retrieved from http://www.johnkay.com/1998/02/03/the-role-of-business-in-society/

Kay, J. (2011). *Obliquity: Why our goals are best achieved indirectly.* Profile Books.

Keating, T. (2009). *Divine Therapy and Addiction.* Lantern Books.

Klein, G. (1999). *Sources of Power: How People Make Decisions.* Cambridge: MIT press.

Krafcik, J. (1988). Triumph of the Lean Production System. *Sloan Management Review, 30*(1).

Krantz, J. (2010). Social Defences and Twenty-First Centure Organizations. *British Journal of Psychotherapy, 26*(2), 192-201.

Law, S. (2011). *Believing Bullshit: How Not to Get Sucked into an Intellectual Black Hole.* Prometheus Books.

Lee, S. (2009, August 5). *Formula From Hell.* Retrieved from Forbes: http://www.forbes.com/2009/05/07/gaussian-copula-david-x-li-opinions-columnists-risk-debt.html

Leiserowitz, Maibach, Roser-Renouf, Feinberg, & Rosenthal. (2015, October). *Climate Change in the American Christian Mind - October 2015.* Retrieved from Yale School of Forestry & Environmental Studies: http://environment.yale.edu/climate-communication/files/Global-Warming-Religion-March-2015.pdf

Li, D. (2000). On Default Correlation: A Copula Function Approach. *Journal of Fixed Income, 9*(4), 43–54.

Luntz, F. (2003). *Luntz memo on the environment.* Retrieved May 28, 2016, from http://www.motherjones.com: http://www.motherjones.com/files/LuntzResearch_environment.pdf

Maibach, E., Myers, T., & Leiserowitz, A. (2014). Climate scientists need to set the record straight: There is a scientific consensus that human-caused climate change is happening. *Earth's Future*.

Maslow, A. (1954). *Motivation and Personality* . Harper & Brothers.

Maslow, A. H. (1943). A Theory of Human Motivation. *Psychological Review, 50*(4), 430-437.

Mathews, P. (2015). Deconstructing management fad adoption: towards a conceptual model. *International Journal of Organizational Analysis, 23*(2), 302 - 319.

McCann, L., Hassard, J. S., Granter, E., & Hyde, P. (2015). Casting the lean spell: The promotion, dilution and erosion of lean management in the NHS. *Human Relations, 68*(10), 1557–1577.

McClelland, D. C. (1953). *The Achievement Motive.* New York: Appleton-Century-Crofts.

McKenna, G. (1988, January). *Discredit The Product.* Retrieved June 6, 2016, from Industry Documents Library: https://www.industrydocumentslibrary.ucsf.edu/tobacco/docs/sznl0100

Mehri, D. (2006). The Darker Side of Lean: An Insider's Perspective on the Realities of the Toyota Production System. *Academy of Management Perspectives, 20*(2), 21-42.

Menzies Lyth, I. E. (1960). A Case-Study in the Functioning of Social Systems as a Defence against Anxiety: A Report on a Study of the Nursing Service of a General Hospital. *Human Relations, 13*(2), 95-121.

Miller, R., & Kowalski, A. (2013, April 17). *Reinhart-Rogoff Paper Cited by Ryan Faulted for 'Serious Flaws'.* Retrieved May 4, 2016, from http://www.bloomberg.com/news/articles/2013-04-16/reinhart-rogoff-paper-cited-by-ryan-faulted-for-serious-errors-

Nelson, R. R. (2015). Physics Envy: Get Over It. *Issues in Science and Technology 31, no. 3.*

Nielsen, J., Zielinski, B., Ferguson, M., Lainhart, J., & Anderson, J. (2013). An Evaluation of the Left-Brain vs. Right-Brain Hypothesis with Resting State Functional Connectivity Magnetic Resonance Imaging. *PLoS ONE*.

Ohno, T. (1988). *Toyota production system: beyond large-scale production*. CRC Press.

Open Science Collaboration. (2015). Estimating the reproducibility of psychological science. *Science, 349*(6251).

Pearce, J. L. (2004). What Do We Know and How Do We Really Know It? *Academy of Management Review, 29*(2), 175-179.

Phelan, S. E. (2001). What Is Complexity Science, Really? *Emergence, 3*(1), 120-136.

Pourdehnad, J., Wilson, D., & Wexler, E. (2011). Systems & Design Thinking: A Conceptual Framework for Their Integration. *Proceedings of the 55th Annual Meeting of the ISSS*. Hull.

Pruijt, H. (2003). Teams between neo-Taylorism and anti-Taylorism. *Economic and Industrial Democracy, 24*(1), 77-101.

Reinhart, C., & Rogoff, K. (2010). Growth in a Time of Debt: Working Paper 15639. *National Bureau of Economic Research*.

Ries, E. (2011). *The Lean Startup: How Today's Entrepreneurs Use Continuous Innovation to Create Radically Successful Businesses*. Crown Business.

Sheldon, K. M. (2001). "What is satisfying about satisfying events? Testing 10 candidate psychological needs. *Journal of personality and social psychology, 80*(2).

Sirota, D., Mischkind, L., & Meltzer, M. (2005). *The Enthusiastic Employee*. Wharton School Publishing.

Smoking and Health Proposal. (1969). Retrieved May 29, 2016, from Truth Tobacco Industry Documents: https://www.industrydocumentslibrary.ucsf.edu/tobacco/docs/#id=psdw0147

Stanovich. (2009). Distinguishing the reflective, algorithmic, and autonomous minds: Is it time for a tri-process theory. In K. Frankish, & Evans, *In Two Minds: Dual Processes and Beyond* (pp. 55-88). Oxford University Press.

Stanovich. (2013). On the Distinction Between Rationality and Intelligence: Implications for Understanding Individual Differences in Reasoning. In K. J. Holyoak, & R. G. Morrison (Eds.), *The Oxford Handbook of Thinking and Reasoning* (p. 433). New York: Oxford University Press.

Stanovich, K. (2012). *How To Think Straight About Psychology.* Pearson; 10 edition (September 29, 2012).

Stanovich, K. (2014). Assessing Cognitive Abilities: Intelligence and More. *Journal of Intelligence,* 8-11.

Stanovich, K. E. (1994). Reconceptualizing intelligence: Dysrationalia as an intuition pump. *Educational Researcher,,* *23*(4), 11-22.

Stanovich, K. E., & West, R. F. (2014). The Assessment of Rational Thinking: IQ ≠ RQ. *Teaching of Psychology, 41*(3), 265-271.

Stanovich, K., & Stanovich, P. (2010). A Framework for Critical Thinking, Rational Thinking, and Intelligence. In R. J. Sternberg, & D. D. Preiss (Eds.), *Innovations in educational psychology: Perspectives on learning, teaching and human development* (pp. 195-237). Springer Publishing Company.

Stoycheva, K. (2011). Intolerance, uncertainty, and individual behaviour in ambiguous situations. In K. Stoycheva, & A. Kostov, *A Place, a Time and an Opportunity for Growth : Bulgarian Scholars at NIAS* (pp. 63-73). FABER Publishing House.

Suzuki, S. (1973). *Zen Mind, Beginner's Mind.* New York, NY, USA: Weatherhill.

Taleb, N. N. (2012). *Antifragile: Things that gain from disorder.* Random House Incorporated.

Taylor, F. (1903). Shop Management. *Transactions of the American Society of Mechanical Engineers, 24,* 1337-1456.

Taylor, F. W. (1911). *The principles of scientific management.* New York & London: Harper Brothers.

Toynbee, P. (2013, April 18). *George Osborne's case for austerity has just started to wobble.* Retrieved May 4, 2016, from The Guardian: http://www.theguardian.com/commentisfree/2013/apr/18/debt-error-bombshell-shatters-austerity

Wastell, D. (1996). The Fetish of Technique: Methodology as a Social Defence. *Information Systems Journal, 6*(1), 25-40.

Webster, D. M., & Kruglanski, A. W. (1994). Individual differences in need for cognitive closure. *Journal of personality and social psychology, 67*(6), 1049.

Welch, S. (2009, March 16). *Jack Welch Elaborates: Shareholder Value.* Retrieved from Bloomberg:

http://www.bloomberg.com/news/articles/2009-03-16/jack-welch-elaborates-shareholder-value

Whitty, S. J. (2005). A memetic paradigm of project management. *International Journal of Project Management, 23*(8), 575-583.

Williamson, O. E. (2010). Transaction Cost Economics: The Natural Progression. *The American Economic Review, 100*(3), 673-690.

Wilson, A. (2014, May 26). *Psychology's real replication problem: our Methods sections.* Retrieved from Notes from Two Scientific Psychologists: http://psychsciencenotes.blogspot.com.au/2014/05/psychologys-real-replication-problem.html

Winnicott, D. (1953). Transitional Objects and Transitional Phenomena. *International Journal of Psychoanalysis*, 89-97.

Index

About the Authors

Paul Culmsee (@paulculmsee) Paul is a management consultant, business strategist, sensemaker and award winning author with more than 25 years of experience. Based in Perth, Western Australia, he co-founded Seven Sigma Business Solutions (www.sevensigma.com.au) and specialises in sensemaking, helping organisations (re)discover their purpose, knowledge management, strategic planning, IT governance, facilitation and all facets of SharePoint and Office365 delivery. Paul is one of only four Cognexus Certified Dialogue Mappers in the world. He and his wife have the best two children in the world and live in Perth, Australia.

Web: http://www.sevensigma.com.au
Blog: http://www.cleverworkarounds.com
Twitter: http://www.twitter.com/paulculmsee
LinkedIn: https://au.linkedin.com/in/paul-culmsee-business-strategist-sensemaker-3555853

Kailash Awati: (@kailashawati) Kailash is co-founder and principal of Sensanalytics, a consultancy specialising in sensemaking and analytics. Prior to this, he worked for a pharmaceutical multinational where he set up a global IT service centre specializing in business intelligence, while initiating and running data analytics projects across the business.

Over the last several years, he has worked as a data and analytics geek; facilitator and sensemaker; data / information architect; project manager and engineering software developer in organisations ranging from startups to established firms. Earlier, in what seems to him like another life, he did research in fluid dynamics and other areas of physics and applied mathematics.

Aside from sensemaking and analytics, his professional interests include knowledge management, project management, risk analysis and emergent (low risk, low cost) approaches to developing new capabilities in organisations.

Kailash lives in Sydney, Australia with his wife and two wonderful children.

Web:	http://www.sensanalytics.com
Blog:	http://eight2late.wordpress.com
Twitter:	http://www.twitter.com/kailashawati
LinkedIn:	https://au.linkedin.com/in/kailash-awati-3517a711

More Publications by the Authors

The Heretics Guide to Best Practices: The *Reality* of Managing Complex Problems in Organisations

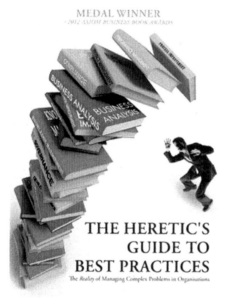

Paul Culmsee and Kailash Awati

When it comes to solving complex problems, we often perform elaborate rituals in the guise of best practices that promise a world of order, certainty, and control. But reality paints a far different picture, which practitioners are often reluctant to discuss. A witty yet rigorous journey through the seedy underbelly of organisational problem solving,

The Heretic's Guide to Best Practices pinpoints the reasons why best practices don't work as advertised and what can be done about it.

Here are some reviewer comments:

"The Heretic's Guide to Best Practices is one of the funniest and most helpful books you could read on how to help groups of people reason together effectively about difficult practical problems. Authors Paul Culmsee and Kailash Awati, whom you may know from their excellent blogs, have written an amazingly clear and conversational guide to the practice of dialogue mapping and collaborative problem structuring."

"The book's discussion of methods for visualizing reasoning is one of the most thought-provoking analyses of this topic that I've read, and I consider myself well read in this area. I would call this book a "must read" for anyone who wants to learn how to create a better world through practical argument mapping or dialogue mapping"

"This should be required reading for consultants, project managers, and anyone else whose job requires building consensus among parties with differing interests and motivations. This book is full of wisdom gleaned from research studies and the authors' experiences, all distilled down to the key findings and presented in an easy to read format. I found myself highlighting much in this book, and I foresee it being a useful reference for years to come"

www.hereticsguidebooks.com

CPSIA information can be obtained
at www.ICGtesting.com
Printed in the USA
LVOW01s2358060417

529957LV00030B/649/P